DATE DUE

FEB 1 0 2012		
JUL 3 1 2012		
APR 2 4 2013		
JAN 0 2 2017		
APR 1 5 2019		

Autism

Psychological Disorders

Psychological Disorders

Autism

Heather Barnett Veague, Ph.D.

Series Editor
Christine Collins, Ph.D.
Research Assistant Professor of Psychology
Vanderbilt University

Foreword by
Pat Levitt, Ph.D.
Director, Vanderbilt Kennedy Center
for Research on Human Development

CHELSEA HOUSE
PUBLISHERS
An imprint of Infobase Publishing

Autism

Chelsea House
An imprint of Infobase Publishing
132 West 31st Street
New York NY 10001

Library of Congress Cataloging-in-Publication Data
Veague, Heather Barnett.
  Autism / Heather Barnett Veague ; consulting editor, Christine Collins ; foreword by Pat Levitt.
      p. cm.
  Includes bibliographical references and index.
  ISBN-13: 978-1-60413-425-4 (hardcover : alk. paper)
  ISBN-10: 1-60413-425-9 (hardcover : alk. paper) 1. Autism—Popular works.
I. Title.
  RC553.A88.V43 2010

  616.85'882—dc22   2009021501

Chelsea House books are available at special discounts when purchased in bulk quantities for businesses, associations, institutions, or sales promotions. Please call our Special Sales Department in New York at (212) 967-8800 or (800) 322-8755.

You can find Chelsea House on the World Wide Web at http://www.chelseahouse.com

Text design by Keith Trego
Cover design by Keith Trego and Alicia Post
Composition by EJB
Cover printed by Bang Printing, Brainerd, MN
Book printed and bound by Bang Printing, Brainerd, MN
Date printed: December 2009
Printed in the United States of America

10 9 8 7 6 5 4 3 2 1

This book is printed on acid-free paper.

All links and Web addresses were checked and verified to be correct at the time of publication. Because of the dynamic nature of the Web, some addresses and links may have changed since publication and may no longer be valid.

Table of Contents

Foreword

Pat Levitt, Ph.D.
Vanderbilt Kennedy
Center for Research
on Human Development

Think of the most complicated aspect of our universe, and then multiply that by infinity! Even the most enthusiastic of mathematicians and physicists acknowledge that the brain is by far the most challenging entity to understand. By design, the human brain is made up of billions of cells called neurons, which use chemical neurotransmitters to communicate with each other through connections called synapses. Each brain cell has about 2,000 synapses. Connections between neurons are not formed in a random fashion, but rather are organized into a type of architecture that is far more complex than any of today's supercomputers. And, not only is the brain's connective architecture more complex than any computer; its connections are capable of *changing* to improve the way a circuit functions. For example, the way we learn new information involves changes in circuits that actually improve performance. Yet some change can also result in a disruption of connections, like changes that occur in disorders such as drug addiction, depression, schizophrenia, and epilepsy, or even changes that can increase a person's risk of suicide.

Genes and the environment are powerful forces in building the brain during development and ensuring normal brain functioning, but they can also be the root causes of psychological and neurological disorders when things go awry. The way in which brain architecture is built before birth and in childhood will determine how well the brain functions when we are adults, and even how susceptible we are to such diseases as depression, anxiety, or attention disorders, which can severely disturb brain function. In a sense, then, understanding how the brain is built can lead us to a clearer picture of the ways in which our brain works, how we can improve its functioning, and what we can do to repair it when diseases strike.

Brain architecture reflects the highly specialized jobs that are performed by human beings, such as seeing, hearing, feeling, smelling, and moving. Different brain areas are specialized to control specific functions. Each specialized area must communicate well with other areas for the brain to accomplish even more complex tasks, like controlling body physiology—our patterns of sleep, for example, or even our eating habits, both of which can become disrupted if brain development or function is disturbed in some way. The brain controls our feelings, fears, and emotions; our ability to learn and store new information; and how well we recall old information. The brain does all this, and more, by building, during development, the circuits that control these functions, much like a hard-wired computer. Even small abnormalities that occur during early brain development through gene mutations, viral infection, or fetal exposure to alcohol can increase the risk of developing a wide range of psychological disorders later in life.

Those who study the relationship between brain architecture and function, and the diseases that affect this bond, are neuroscientists. Those who study and treat the disorders that are caused by changes in brain architecture and chemistry are psychiatrists and psychologists. Over the last 50 years, we have learned quite a lot about how brain architecture and chemistry work and how genetics contributes to brain structure and function. Genes are very important in controlling the initial phases of building the brain. In fact, almost every gene in the human genome is needed to build the brain. This process of brain development actually starts prior to birth, with almost all the neurons we will ever have in our brain produced by mid-gestation. The assembly of the architecture, in the form of intricate circuits, begins by this time, and by birth we have the basic organization laid out. But the work is not yet complete because billions of connections form over a remarkably long period of time, extending through puberty. The brain of a child is being built and modified on a daily basis, even during sleep.

While there are thousands of chemical building blocks, such as proteins, lipids, and carbohydrates, that are used much like bricks and mortar to put the architecture together, the highly detailed connectivity that emerges during childhood depends greatly upon experiences and our environment. In building a house, we use specific blueprints to assemble the basic structures, like a foundation, walls, floors, and ceilings. The brain is assembled similarly. Plumbing and electricity, like the basic circuitry of the brain, are put in place early in the building process. But for all of this early work, there is another very important phase of development, which is termed experience-dependent development. During the first three years of life, our brains actually form far more connections than we will ever need, almost 40 percent more! Why would this occur? Well, in fact, the early circuits form in this way so that we can use experience to mold our brain architecture to best suit the functions that we are likely to need for the rest of our lives

Experience is not just important for the circuits that control our senses. A young child who experiences toxic stress, like physical abuse, will have his or her brain architecture changed in regions that will result in poorer control of emotions and feelings as an adult. Experience is powerful. When we repeatedly practice on the piano or shoot a basketball hundreds of times daily, we are using experience to model our brain connections to function at their finest. Some will achieve better results than others, perhaps because the initial phases of circuit-building provided a better base, just like the architecture of houses may differ in terms of their functionality. We are working to understand the brain structure and function that result from the powerful combination of genes building the initial architecture and a child's experience adding the all-important detailed touches. We also know that, like an old home, the architecture can break down. The aging process can be particularly hard on the ability of brain circuits to function at their best because positive change comes less readily as we get older. Synapses may be lost and brain chemistry can change over time. The difficulties in understanding how architecture gets built are paralleled by the complexities of what happens to that architecture as we grow older. Dementia associated with brain deterioration as a complication of Alzheimer's disease and memory loss associated with aging or alcoholism are active avenues of research in the neuroscience community.

There is truth, both for development and in aging, in the old adage "use it or lose it." Neuroscientists are pursuing the idea that brain architecture and chemistry can be modified well beyond childhood. If we understand the mechanisms that make it easy for a young, healthy brain to learn or repair itself following an accident, perhaps we can use those same tools to optimize the functioning of aging brains. We already know many ways in which we can improve the functioning of the aging or injured brain. For example, for an individual who has suffered a stroke that has caused structural damage to brain architecture, physical exercise can be quite powerful in helping to reorganize circuits so that they function better, even in an elderly individual. And you know that when you exercise and sleep regularly, you just feel better. Your brain chemistry and architecture are functioning at their best. Another example of ways we can improve nervous system function are the drugs that are used to treat mental illnesses. These drugs are designed to change brain chemistry so that the neurotransmitters used for communication between brain cells can function more normally. These same types of drugs, however, when taken in excess or abused, can actually damage brain chemistry and change brain architecture so that it functions more poorly.

As you read the Psychological Disorders series, the images of altered brain organization and chemistry will come to mind in thinking about complex diseases such as schizophrenia or drug addiction. There is nothing more fascinating and important to understand for the well-being of humans. But also keep in mind that as neuroscientists, we are on a mission to comprehend human nature, the way we perceive the world, how we recognize color, why we smile when thinking about the Thanksgiving turkey, the emotion of experiencing our first kiss, or how we can remember the winner of the 1953 World Series. If you are interested in people, and the world in which we live, you are a neuroscientist, too.

Pat Levitt, Ph.D.
Director, Vanderbilt Kennedy Center
for Research on Human Development
Vanderbilt University
Nashville, Tennessee

What Is Autism?

Brian, age 10, was referred to a psychologist after his public school could no longer meet his educational needs. Brian's mother, Jane, is very worried about him. Brian has always been different from other children. Shortly after his first birthday, Brian seemed to lose interest in other people. His exhibited poor eye contact and his focus was often on his mother's shiny earrings rather than on her face. Brian was a bit slow to develop speech, although his physical milestones (crawling, walking) were met with ease. Jane did not enroll Brian in preschool until he was five years old. She believed he was too shy, and as a result, he was kept at home for most of his early years.

When Brian started school, it immediately became clear that he was "of his own mind." His grandmother knew this, and encouraged Jane to take him to get help right away. Jane feared what would happen if Brian was labeled with a mental disorder as a child, so she fought to keep him in the public school and tutored him herself to help his achievement remain consistent with his peers. From kindergarten through fourth grade, Brian struggled both socially and academically. He had no friends, and his teachers appeared to be annoyed by him. He would often speak out of turn, and did not seem to be able to learn how to consistently follow directions. He occasionally made rude comments about others' appearance and was surprised when he was scolded for what seemed to him to be a normal observation. At age eight, Brian continued having problems controlling his bladder and bowels. Accidents were not uncommon, and Brian's mother dealt with this by having her son wear feminine hygiene products under his clothes. By the time he was 10, the principal at Brian's school told Jane that they could no longer meet Brian's needs, and Jane conceded. She took Brian to see a therapist who specialized in developmental problems.

Surprisingly, Brian was not bothered about leaving his school. He was not attached to anyone there, and was only concerned when the therapist raised the idea of Brian going to a residential educational community—a boarding school for children with developmental problems. However, Brian was not concerned about leaving his mother; rather he worried about leaving his extensive train set that he had been collecting and playing with for years. It appeared that Brian was more attached to his train set than to his family. Jane was not surprised. She was used to Brian's emotional distance. Still, part of her was sad to realize that her son was so far away from her, despite all her efforts to keep him close.

Relationships with family and friends are extremely important to most people. Even as infants, human beings can tell their caregivers how they feel by smiling, laughing, fussing, or crying. Similarly, babies use other people's emotional signals—their facial expressions, body language, or words—to figure out how they are feeling. These skills come so easily to most of us that we often take them for granted. Imagine what your life would be like if you could not understand what your mother meant when she smiled. Imagine if you had difficulty understanding your own feelings, and were unable to put those feelings into words. People with autistic disorder have these kinds of problems. People with autism are challenged by social and behavioral problems that affect their ability to communicate with others.

According to recent prevalence estimates by the National Institute of Mental Health, autism affects between .003 and .006 percent of the population. This means that out of every

Figure 1.1 Babies use other people's emotional signals—facial expressions, body language, or words—to figure out how others are feeling. Children with an autistic disorder have trouble reading these signals and may appear indifferent to social cues. (© Shutterstock)

1,000 children, between 3 and 6 of them will have the disorder. Further, males are four times more likely than females to have autism. This means that for every girl with autism, four boys have the disorder. It is unclear exactly why boys are more likely to develop autism than girls, but you can read more about the gender differences in Chapter 3.

Autism is a **heterogeneous** disorder. That means that people with autism can look and act very different from one another. Brian, the young boy described at the beginning of this chapter, is moderately affected by autism. His intelligence is average, but his social skills are significantly impaired; Brian's disruptive behavior limits his educational opportunities. Some people with autism are so impaired that they must have help with even their most basic needs, such as eating, dressing, or going to the bathroom. Indeed, Brian's ability to care for himself is compromised, as demonstrated by his inability to consistently control his bladder and bowels. Other people with autism can function quite well, live independently, maintain relationships, and work at high-level jobs. Because of the vast difference in severity among those with autism, identification and treatment programs are constantly changing. Clinicians and researchers are pressed to develop new screening tools and treatment programs to meet the needs of a diverse population.

CASE STUDY

Marcus is seven. He lives with his parents, John and Sarah, and his older sister Lucy. Marcus was diagnosed with autism when he was two-and-a-half. His pediatrician had referred his family to a child psychologist, who observed that his social and communication skills were significantly delayed. John and Sarah were devastated. They realized that Marcus was slow, particularly compared to their daughter Lucy, but they just assumed that he was taking his time. "Boys are different," Sarah would say.

Shortly after receiving the diagnosis, Marcus began demonstrating some disturbing behavior. He developed an alarming attachment to a set of measuring cups. He lined these cups up over and over again, usually stacking them one on top of another, but occasionally putting them into rows by decreasing size. When Sarah tried to take the cups away to use them to bake some cookies, Marcus screamed, threw a tantrum, and banged his head repeatedly against the floor. Sarah was terrified. She held Marcus tightly, trying to keep him from hurting himself. Unfortunately, this made things worse. Marcus flailed and fought back to be left alone, as if he could not stand to be touched. Finally, after he wore himself out, Marcus went to sleep and Sarah called the psychologist. She enrolled Marcus in a special school where he is taught to control his behaviors and care for his basic needs.

Every day, Marcus goes to school and works one-on-one with a therapist. At age seven, his language is limited, and he still has no friends nor does he truly connect with his family. However, he knows how to get himself dressed, feed himself, and use the bathroom. His tantrums can be frightening, but Sarah and John know how to avoid them and try to deal with them appropriately when they do occur. They know that Marcus faces challenges and will likely continue to face challenges throughout his life. They are committed to finding him the support he needs and to bridging the communication gap they have with their son.

Autism affects more people than just those who have the disorder. Their loved ones must deal with the disappointment, alienation, and confusion that can come with caring for a person with autism. Marcus's parents, Sarah and John, were forced to make changes to their own behavior in order to adapt to life with an autistic son. Autism is a challenge to everyone who comes into contact with it, and it is important to understand the symptoms, the origin, and the treatment of autism. Autism, by definition, is an alienating disorder. People who have the disorder show deficits in two areas: social interaction and verbal and nonverbal communication. This means that someone with autism may have limited social skills as well as difficulty understanding the social cues of others. Additionally, many people with autism have unusual, repetitive, or severely limited activities and interests. In children, this might appear as a preference for a certain toy. Like Marcus and his measuring cups, a child with autism may become so preoccupied with a certain toy or

Figure 1.2 Children with autism lack interest in the outside world and exhibit poor social skills. *(© Doctor Kan/Shutterstock)*

type of play that it appears obsessive. Caregivers usually notice the symptoms or signs of autism in children under the age of two. However, like Marcus's parents, it can be challenging for parents and health professionals to determine what behaviors are signs of autism and what can be explained by simply a small deviation from normal development. Some symptoms of autism can also be indications of other types of mental illness. In order to confirm a diagnosis of autism, treatment professionals will consider all **disorders first identified in childhood**, also known as **pervasive developmental disorders.**

Pervasive developmental disorders appear when children exhibit severe and pervasive impairment in several areas of development including social skills, communication, or repetitive or **stereotyped** behavior, interests or activities. Children with these types of problems must appear distinctly different from other children their age; specifically, their development must be significantly delayed as compared to their peers. In addition to autistic disorder, pervasive developmental disorders include Rett's disorder, childhood disintegrative disorder, and **Asperger syndrome**. Oftentimes, children with these disorders also have some degree of mental retardation. Alternatively, many children with pervasive developmental disorders may have normal or above average intelligence.

The presentation of developmental disorders can vary greatly. Rett's disorder occurs only in females. Girls with Rett's disorder appear normal at birth and for the first five months. Problems begin to emerge between five months and four years of age, during which head growth slows down and motor and social skills may be lost. Similarly, childhood disintegrative disorder is characterized by normal development for the first two years of life followed by a regression, or loss of social and communication skills. Finally, Asperger syndrome is sometimes considered a mild form of autism. Children with Asperger syndrome have problems in social interaction and restricted interests in activities, but lack the speech delay often seen in autism. Further, people with Asperger syndrome demonstrate normal intellectual development and are able to care for themselves in ways appropriate to their age. All of these disorders appear in childhood, but their effects continue into adulthood. Each child develops differently—those with mental disorders and those without. As a result, clinicians who work with kids who have pervasive developmental disorders do their best to consider each child individually and make diagnostic and treatment decisions accordingly.

(*continues on page 10*)

The Autistic Savant

The term "savant" generally refers to someone with scholarly learning, someone gifted. It includes skills that are in direct contrast to what we think of when we think of someone with autism. However, about 10 percent of autistic people develop savant skills. Precise skills, be they musical, artistic, or mathematical are particularly unusual when coupled with the problems associated with autism. Darold Treffert at the University of Wisconsin–Madison Medical School has identified three levels of savant syndrome. Splinter skills, the most common form of savant skill, include obsessive preoccupation and memorization of facts and trivia. Areas of expertise might include historical facts, sports statistics, or music trivia. The second most common, the talented savant, is someone who has an expertise in music, art, or math that's particularly remarkable given his or her disability. A prodigious savant is extremely rare (there are likely less than 50 in the world)[1], has skills so outstanding that they would be amazing even in a non-autistic person. An example of an extremely rare savant skill is calendar counting. Calendar counting is the ability to name the day of the week that a particular date falls several years in the future. Someone who can calendar count may be able to tell you the years in which Christmas will fall on a Saturday.

The movie *Rain Man*, starring Tom Cruise and Dustin Hoffman was the story of two brothers, one a selfish yuppie (Cruise) and the other an autistic savant (Hoffman). Dustin Hoffman's character was based on the real life savant Kim Peek. Although it is now debated whether Peek is truly autistic or suffers from some other form of developmental disability, his savant skills go unchallenged. According to Peek's father, Kim was able to memorize things from before he was two years old. When he began reading, he would read books and then place them upside down on a shelf to show that he had finished it. His recall is remarkable as he apparently remembers about 98% of everything he has ever read. He can recall the content of more than 10,000 books. Peek has been the subject of a great deal of study, including studies using brain imaging techniques in order to reveal structural or functional brain differences that might explain his unusual abilities.

Another savant who has received a great deal of attention in the popular media is Daniel Tammet. Tammet was born in 1979 in the United Kingdom. When he was a small child, Tammet suffered an epileptic seizure, which apparently left him with some remarkable savant skills. The title of his memoir, *Born on a Blue Day*, refers to his association of colors with days of the week. Synesthesia occurs when one thought (like a number, word, or day of the week) is automatically and unconsciously paired with a sensation such as a color, smell, or feeling. Synesthesia is extremely rare, and understood only vaguely as a neurologically based phenomenon. Daniel Tammet is affected by Asperger syndrome, synesthesia and epilepsy. His savant skills include a remarkable ability for learning languages (he speaks 11 languages and has created one of his own) as well as mathematical genius. He holds the world record for the recitation of Pi to 22,514 digits in five hours and nine minutes. What is particularly astounding about Daniel Tammet is that he appears to be able to explain how he performs his savant skills. Tammet is helping researchers understand how savant skills work, as well as gain insight into the internal life of people with autism spectrum disorders.

(*continued from page 7*)

THE AUTISM SPECTRUM

For many clinicians and researchers, autism is best described using a **spectrum approach**. Using a spectrum approach assures that we view autism on a **continuum**. A continuum is a progression of values, in this case symptoms, which ranges from low or few symptoms, to high, or many symptoms. Someone on the low end of the autism spectrum will have few symptoms of the disorder, whereas someone on the other end of the continuum will have severe autism. Consider the two case studies described above. The severity of Brian's illness might put him to the low to middle end of the autism spectrum. In contrast, Marcus would likely fall on the high end.

Asperger syndrome is sometimes called **high-functioning autism**. By definition, someone with Asperger syndrome has problems interacting and communicating with other people. They might have poor eye contact or unusual ways of speaking. Someone with Asperger syndrome may have problems with humor and have difficulty understanding simple jokes. In addition, someone with Asperger syndrome will show almost obsessive interests in specific activities. They might be experts on something like astronomy or mathematics. Topics with complicated patterns allow someone with Asperger syndrome to work alone for extended periods of time. In Chapter 4 you will read about John Robison, a man with Asperger syndrome who has become a very successful mechanic of high-end cars. Someone with Asperger syndrome could be an excellent mechanic. Intent on understanding how things work, a mechanic with Asperger syndrome would work diligently to fix a car. Luckily for his or her customers, people with Asperger syndrome are unlikely to lie; they are usually honest to a fault, and as a result will only perform necessary work.

Unlike autism, Asperger syndrome is not characterized by speech or cognitive delays. Children with Asperger syndrome will develop at a rate similar to kids without autism in every way other than social skills. Although many children are shy and may have problems making friends, a child with Asperger syndrome is either uninterested in making friends or lacks an understanding of how to interact with their peers. Being able to share in one's feelings, like being happy for a friend, is called **emotional reciprocity**. A child with Asperger syndrome lacks emotional reciprocity, and as a result is challenged when it comes to making friendships or interacting with peers.

Recently, the autism diagnosis has received a great deal of attention in the popular media. Some people believe that there is an **epidemic** of autism. An epidemic occurs when cases of a disease appear in a human population at a rate that is greater than what would be expected. Indeed, the number of children diagnosed with autism appears to be growing. However, the reasons behind the growing number of diagnosed cases of autism are complicated. There are some groups that talk about childhood vaccinations as being a cause of autism. Others believe that a certain diet can "cure" autism. There are several myths surrounding the **etiology**, or causes, and treatment of autism. One must take a critical approach and investigate all sides of the argument in order to understand what makes a child become autistic and what we can do to treat it and prevent new cases from emerging.

Psychiatric diagnoses are imperfect categories. Like any physical disease, people with a mental illness may show a variety of signs or symptoms. In order to diagnose a mental illness, one must exhibit a certain number of symptoms. Sometimes one or more symptoms are required for the diagnosis. For autism, this is delayed speech and impaired social skills. However, one person with autism might rock his body back and forth for hours, whereas another child might just be extremely withdrawn and concentrate on a train set. When researchers obtain more information about a disorder, they might change the description of the category, or the diagnosis. When this happens, new cases of the disorder may be identified. Other times, people who previously received the diagnosis no longer meet the criteria for the disorder. When a diagnosis changes, the number of people who have the disorder changes as well. In order to determine whether or not there is a true epidemic of autism, we need to consider how the diagnosis has changed over the corresponding time frame. Specifically, we must ask ourselves whether there are more actual cases of autism now, compared to 20 years ago, or if clinicians are simply better at identifying the disorder. You will read a detailed discussion about what is contributing to the "autism epidemic" in Chapter 6.

● ● ● ● ● ● ● ●

SUMMARY

Autism is a disorder characterized by impaired social and emotional skills. It appears in childhood and continues into adulthood. Because autism is a heterogeneous disorder, it is best understood using a spectrum approach. In Chapter 2, you will read about who develops autism. Chapter 3 will cover the causes of autism. In Chapter 4 you will learn about the treatment and outcome of people who have autism. Asperger syndrome is the topic of Chapter 5. Finally, in Chapter 6 you will learn about the debate surrounding the "epidemic" of autism.

Identifying Autism

2

Rose is a beautiful three-year-old child. Strangers often comment on her golden curls and bright blue eyes and say she looks like a porcelain doll. Rose is so beautiful in fact that she receives a great deal of attention in the outside world. This makes Rose very uncomfortable. Although she has a few words—"milk," "Charlie" (her dog), and "no"— she only uses them at home with her parents, Theo and Alexandra. Rose is virtually mute outside of her home. Her parents, both social and outgoing people, wonder why Rose is so different from them. Until recently, they have ignored her efforts to stay home. They believe that Rose simply needs more experience with other people to overcome her shyness. Lately, however, Theo and Alexandra have begun to acknowledge that something might be wrong.

On Rose's third birthday medical checkup with Dr. Watson, her mother filled out a form detailing Rose's development over the past year. Dr. Watson was alarmed at how little progress Rose had made. He asked Rose several questions but did not receive any answers. In fact, Rose never made eye contact with Dr. Watson. At the end of the exam, Rose was scheduled to receive two vaccinations. Her mother hesitated because she had heard rumors that some vaccinations might cause autism. Dr. Watson assured her that data supported the safety of the vaccines and Rose's mother complied. When the nurse entered to administer the shots, Rose sat very still and silent. She objected more to the nurse holding her arm than to the prick of the needle. In sum, the exam caused Dr. Watson and Alexandra to worry. Dr. Watson asked Alexandra to come back with her husband for a meeting.

Two weeks later, Theo and Alexandra returned to the pediatrician's office for a meeting. In addition to Dr. Watson, Dr. May, a child psychologist, was in the room. Dr. May specialized in developmental disorders. Dr. May asked Alexandra and Theo several questions. Did Rose respond to her name? Did Rose make eye contact with her parents? How about with her peers? Did Rose like to be cuddled? When Rose did speak, did she use words like "I" or "me" or did she refer to herself in the third person? Did Rose show an unusual favoritism for a specific type of alone play? Theo and Alexandra were alarmed. Most of the questions Dr. May asked introduced concerns. They wondered what this meant and what they could do.

A plan was made to thoroughly examine Rose. Dr. May wanted to have Rose's hearing tested first to rule out any impairment. Rose would have a series of cognitive tests to determine if there was any delay, mental retardation, or learning disability. After ruling these problems out, Rose might have an MRI to be certain that there were no tumors or neurological abnormalities that might account for her behavior. After the initial battery of cognitive and neurological examinations, Dr. May will talk to Rose and watch her play. With patience and luck, Dr. May will be able to figure out whether Rose has a pervasive developmental disorder, like autism, and determine the most appropriate course of treatment.

Parents are usually the first to notice signs of autism in their children. Some parents recall that their child always seemed "different" from other children. Other parents report that their once happy, babbling toddler became oddly quiet and withdrawn. If a child appears consistently silent, indifferent to social cues, or self-abusive they might be showing behaviors that indicate autism. If this occurs, parents are encouraged to consult a treatment professional, such as a child psychologist, in order to confirm or rule out the diagnosis.

HISTORY OF AUTISM

Autism is a relatively new disorder. Unlike schizophrenia, which was identified more than 100 years ago, autism was not formally identified until 1943. Dr. Leo Kanner at Johns Hopkins Hospital in Maryland is credited with the first structured description of autistic children. Kanner studied 11 children who exhibited poor social skills, self-abuse, and repetitive or stereotyped patterns of behavior and named this phenomenon "early infantile autism."

Because of the apparent self-absorption of autistic children, early theorists considered autism a form of schizophrenia. In 1910, Eugen Bleuler, a pioneer in schizophrenia research, first used the term *autism* to refer to schizophrenia symptoms. The word *autism* derives from the Latin root *auto*, meaning "self"— this refers to the morbid self-absorption of patients with schizophrenia. Thirty years later, Dr. Kanner used the term to identify his young patients, referring to their lack of interest in the outside, social world. Indeed, until the middle of the twentieth century, autism was generally considered a form of childhood schizophrenia. This caused many problems for patients and their families. Early forms of treatment for autism invariably involved placing the child in an institution. Treatment vaguely focused on teaching autistic children speech through imitation, but most efforts went toward containing their self-abusive behaviors, rather than on rehabilitation. In the 1960s and 1970s some experimental medications, including the now-illicit drug **lysergic acid diethylamide (LSD)**, were used unsuccessfully to treat autism. Other therapies included **electro-convulsive treatment (ECT)**, colloquially known as shock therapy. ECT, while sometimes effective for severe mood disorders, did little more

Figure 2.1 Dr. Leo Kanner, above, is credited with the first structured description of autistic children. *(National Library of Medicine/ U.S. National Institutes of Health)*

than tranquilize people with autism and was later largely dismissed as a treatment option. Early treatment for autism was viewed much like treatment for many mental disorders. Present approaches to autism treatment are quite different.

Other treatments for autism have focused on behavior and environment. In 1944, American psychologist Bruno Bettlcheim, at the University of Chicago's Orthogenic School, established a new theory for the etiology of autism as well as a corresponding treatment method. Bettleheim's theory essentially blamed the parents of autistic children for the disorder, coining the term "refrigerator mother" to refer to the coldness with which mothers of autistic children allegedly raised their children. His theory was largely debunked by the 1980s and 1990s, although a few practitioners and theorists still believe parenting styles have something to do with the disorder. However, Bettleheim's treatment methods were rumored to have some success in treating emotionally disturbed children. He used **milieu therapy**, a treatment approach that establishes an environment that is rich with real life experiences and opportunities for positive social interactions and feedback from caring staff members. Structure, social reward, and an empathic staff are essential to milieu therapy, and it continues today as an effective treatment for many types of mental disorders. You will read more about treatment options for the autism spectrum disorders in Chapter 4.

DEMOGRAPHICS: WHO DEVELOPS AUTISM?

In general, autism appears to affect different groups of people equally. Racial identity, ethnic group, and **socioeconomic status** do not influence who is more likely to develop autism. Alternatively, three factors can increase the likelihood that a child will develop autism. To begin, boys are much more likely to have autism. Statistics show that boys are three to four times more likely to develop autism than girls.[1] Autism appears to run in families. A younger sibling of an autistic child has a risk of between 2 and 8 percent of developing autism. This rate is much higher than for the general population. Finally, some genetic conditions often occur in addition to autism. Whether

Figure 2.2 Boys are three to four times more likely to develop autism than girls. (© Aleksey Kondratyuk/Shutterstock)

the genetic condition is the cause of autistic behaviors or independent of these behaviors must be determined by a medical professional. For example, mental retardation and **Fragile X syndrome** might be complicated by a diagnosis of autism. Fragile X syndrome is the most common cause of inherited mental impairment. It is caused by **gene** changes in the FRM1 gene. Fragile X is the most common cause of autistic-like behaviors in people. Although Fragile X includes a whole host of problems including physical and cognitive impairment, its connection to autism does not occur in all carriers of the gene. Autistic people are often screened for Fragile X, and vice versa, in order to make the most accurate diagnosis and treatment plan.

HOW DO AUTISTIC CHILDREN UNDERSTAND THEIR WORLD?

In a sense, we are all mind readers. We are mind readers in that we can sometimes interpret what others are thinking or feeling. People often give us clues as to their thoughts and feelings. Perhaps your best friend blushes when you accidentally tell her secret in the cafeteria. You know that you have done something that has hurt her feelings, or made her embarrassed. You immediately apologize, or maybe make a joke to distract the others, or change the subject. The fact is that you sense that other people feel different from you and you can adjust your behavior accordingly.

A **theory of mind** is the ability to attribute others' mental states (like beliefs, thoughts, or feelings) and use that information to inform or predict behavior. A classic experiment illustrating the theory of mind is the **false-belief task** first developed by Heinz Wimmer and Josef Perner in 1983. The simplest version of this task is the Sally–Anne game. A child is told to watch a story unfold about two girls. One girl, Sally, puts a chocolate into a drawer and leaves the room. Anne then comes into the room, opens the drawer, takes the chocolate and puts it in a cupboard. Then Sally returns to the room. The child is then asked where Sally will look for the chocolate. Someone with a theory of mind knows that Sally will look in the drawer, where she put the chocolate in the first place. Sally did not see Anne come in and move the chocolate, thus her belief should be consistent with her own behavior. Children without a theory of mind know that the chocolate is now in the cupboard and will assume that Sally also knows that the chocolate has been moved. Researchers generally agree that the theory of mind does not emerge until age three or four. Children with autism spectrum disorder find this task particularly challenging. By definition, autism is marked by an inability to interpret others' behaviors and a lack of perspective-taking. The development of theory of mind is delayed—and occasionally absent—in people with autism spectrum disorders. However, some integrative therapies for autistic people focus on learning perspective-taking and understanding how others might have a point of view that differs from one's own. Although understanding that other people think differently from you may be easy for most people, autistic people struggle daily with decoding the intentions of others.

AUTISM IN ADULTS

Autism is a pervasive developmental disorder. This means that: (1) autism is diagnosed in childhood; and (2) autism affects the way in which children's cognitive and social skills develop. What does this mean for the autistic adult? Does autism continue across the lifespan or does it "get better" as we age? Unfortunately, autism is a lifelong condition. That is not to say that someone with autism cannot learn to live with its challenges. Early intervention, a good educational foundation, and a strong support network can help adults with autism learn to live satisfying and productive lives.

Autistic adults fall into two categories: low-functioning and high-functioning. Low-functioning autistic people need a lot of services. They will likely live at home with their families or in a residential setting designed to help people with mental disorders. The goal for low-functioning autistic adults is to manage their basic life skills, like feeding oneself, taking care of personal hygiene and refraining from self-harm. Adults with moderate or high-functioning autism have a greater opportunity for independent living than low-functioning autistic people. They are often able to find meaningful work in a mainstream occupation. However, social interactions will continue to be problematic for them. Other people with autism might find work in the general population daunting. For these folks, work in a structured

Figure 2.3 Workers at this support center for autistic adults teach them to cook, helping individuals to become more independent. *(© AP Images)*

environment, under the direction of someone trained in dealing with people with developmental disorders can be fulfilling. Organizations like Community Services for Autistic Adults and Children (CSAAC) can help connect autistic adults with support groups, residential centers, and occupational opportunities in their community.

In most states, public education for people with disabilities ends by the age of 22. Fortunately, social services exist to help adults with their particular life challenges. Unfortunately, the burden for arranging for care for an autistic adult often falls on the family. This can be both emotionally and financially challenging. Federal funds can help ease the burden for families with

(continues on page 24)

Temple Grandin

Observation is the way we usually learn about mental illness. Clinicians or researchers will interview or observe individuals with disordered behaviors, record these observations, and they will form the foundation of our understanding about specific disorders. Autism is a particularly difficult disorder to understand because by definition, people with autism lack communication and social skills. As a result, we know very little about what it is like to be autistic. The experience of autism is difficult for most of us to understand or imagine.

Temple Grandin is autistic and has written several books about her experience living with autism. Grandin did not speak until age three-and-a-half and instead communicated by screaming, humming, and peeping. Thanks to a determined mother, gifted and compassionate teachers, and her own innate curiosity and intellect, Grandin eventually learned to communicate with others and learn how to live in a "neurotypical," or non-autistic, world. In her book, *Emergence: Labeled Autistic*, Grandin describes learning to live with autism when the diagnosis left little hope for others with the disorder.

One of Temple Grandin's most impressive characteristics is her insight into autism. She is able to identify ways in which she is different from others and create rules or solutions for dealing in a society that she sometimes struggles to understand. From infancy, Grandin was overstimulated by human touch. Still, she craved the calming pressure of an embrace. In *Emergence: Labeled Autistic*, Grandin describes her search for the perfect "hug:"

> When I outgrew wrapping myself in a blanket or crawl-
> ing under a sofa pillow, I tried to figure out another

Figure 2.4 Temple Grandin. *(© AP Images)*

means for pleasant stimulation. Maybe some sort of machine . . .

While daydreaming during class in the third grade, I visualized a different kind of comfort machine. This design was sort of a coffin-like box. I imagined crawling in the open end. Once inside, I would lay on my back, inflate a plastic lining, which would hold me tightly but ever so gently. And most importantly, even in my imagination, I controlled the amount of pressure exerted by the plastic lining."[2]

As an adolescent, Grandin learned about cattle restraints at her aunt's ranch in Arizona. For Grandin, this began to illuminate the connection between animal and human psychology.

(continues)

(continued)

Cattle restraints are used to keep animals still during veterinary procedures. At the same time, they have a calming effect on cattle. Grandin observed this calming effect and designed her own "hug machine" or "squeeze box." This is a large contraption in which a person can lie and have pressure applied to the sides of his or her body. Grandin found that her prototype hug machine helped her deal with her intense anxiety. Today a version of the machine is manufactured and used for treatment for autistic people worldwide.

Working with animals has always been therapeutic for Grandin. Even as an adolescent, Grandin preferred spending time with horses than with humans. After pursuing a college degree in psychology, Grandin completed her Ph.D. in animal science at the University of Illinois and has become an expert in cattle handling and humane slaughter. Her autism, according to Grandin, allows her to understand animals' anxiety. As a result, she has designed slaughterhouses in a way in which the animals stress level and natural behaviors are taken into consideration. Today Grandin is a professor of animal science at Colorado State University and a consultant to companies including Burger King and McDonald's.

(*continued from page 21*)

a member with autism. Social Security Disability Insurance (SSDI) benefits or Supplemental Security Income (SSI) can be a lifesaver for some families. Connecting autistic people with these resources takes time and often requires the assistance of a professional. Social workers and developmental specialists can help families secure financial support for their children.

Like autistic children, adults with autism can learn to live with their particular challenges. The non-autistic world may be an uncomfortable place for adults with autism. People have expectations of appropriate social interactions and someone with autism usually fails to understand or meet those expectations. As with any mental illness, a strong support network of family, educators, and treatment professionals can ease the transition into adulthood and living day to day with a developmental disorder.

WHAT IS A PSYCHIATRIC DIAGNOSIS?

Deciding whether or not someone has a mental disorder is an important and challenging job. Though having a diagnosis of a mental disorder may help one ultimately gain access to valuable treatment programs, it can also lead to stereotyping and discrimination. A **stereotype** is an assumption about someone based solely upon that person's membership in a particular group. Like members of racial or ethnic groups, people with mental illness can also be the target of stereotyping. Unfortunately, stereotyping can lead to prejudice and unfair treatment. People who are the victim of negative stereotypes often report feelings of depression and low self-esteem. For someone living with mental illness, having to cope with discrimination can be even more disabling than the diagnosis.

Prejudice and stereotyping can also serve to elicit or maintain disordered behaviors. **Labeling theory** is the idea that labels used to describe one's behavior can actually affect how that person behaves. Howard Becker, a University of Chicago-trained sociologist, is generally accepted as the man who developed the ideas behind labeling theory, which has primarily been applied to people who engage in criminal behavior. According to labeling theory, someone who is identified as a criminal by the criminal justice system is more likely to engage in further criminal behavior simply as a result of the social reaction he encounters as a criminal. To illustrate, consider Bob, a man who was incarcerated for five years for burglary. When Bob gets out of prison he calls his old friends and learns that they want nothing to do with him anymore. Bob tries to get a job but must report on all job applications that he has a criminal record and as a result, Bob cannot get a job. Without a job, Bob cannot support himself. He feels despondent and hopeless and ultimately returns to criminal behavior to survive. Though Bob indeed committed a crime and deserved to go to prison, he finds life on the outside even more challenging. His label of criminal now defines him and ultimately drives his behavior.

Labeling theory has also been applied to the mentally ill. Strict labeling theorists believe that there is no such thing as mental illness. Instead, they argue that society creates an idea of what is normal and when someone behaves in a way that differs from the norm, we view them as disordered. A diagnosis, or a label, has two results. First, when we are told that a new classmate has autism, we expect him or her to act differently from us. As a result, we might treat that classmate differently. Perhaps we treat the classmate gently, assuming that he or she needs our help. Alternatively, we might treat them harshly or we ignore them altogether. Second, the new classmate grows accustomed to being helped, insulted, or ignored and lowers his or her own expectations. Labeling theory posits that the diagnosis, or the label, can then perpetuate behaviors that would not be there otherwise.

There is a vocal minority of psychological researchers and clinicians who feel very strongly that diagnosis harms people. Unfortunately, for now, there are no alternatives that allow for people with mental illness to be identified and treated. Some theorists believe that a continuum model, as opposed to a categorical model, better serves those with a mental illness.

You read about the continuum model of autism, or the autism spectrum. The continuum model can also be applied to mental illness in general. The idea of a continuum model is that all behaviors appear in the population on a continuum. Consider, for example, riding on roller coasters. **Sensation-seeking behavior** is behavior that a person engages in to get a physical rush, a feeling of euphoria or excitement. Some people love to ride on roller coasters. They love to feel out of control, and the adrenaline rush they get is very rewarding to them. For others, a roller coaster is terrifying. The anxiety they get just waiting in line to board the roller coaster is almost unbearable. Unfortunately, the same sensation-seeking tendencies that lead one to enjoy roller coasters can also lead them to use illicit drugs. These behaviors, in the extreme, can cause a person to have real challenges in leading a productive life. If the sensation-seeking urge trumps all other behaviors, the sensation seeker on the high end of the sensation-seeking continuum might engage in behaviors (like drug use) that significantly impair their lives. On the opposite end of the spectrum are people who are terrified of roller coasters, or people who are low on the sensation-seeking continuum. These are people who might be more fearful by nature and are prone to anxiety. If their fear or anxiety becomes disruptive to their lives (perhaps keeping them from leaving the house), they could use help learning to manage their anxiety. Proponents of the continuum approach to mental illness argue that the model would prevent people from being burdened with the negative judgments that can accompany a psychiatric diagnosis.

The debate surrounding the utility of psychiatric diagnosis continues to this day. Practitioners who work with children are especially cautious in assigning diagnoses to their students or patients. Still, most clinicians and researchers agree that they

(*continues on page 30*)

Synesthesia

For most of us, a word is a word and a smell is a smell. That is, our senses are segregated—functioning alone and without interference from our thoughts. For people with synesthesia, one stimulus may share characteristics with another totally unrelated stimulus. Synesthesia, from the ancient Greek meaning "together sensation," occurs when the stimulation of one sensory pathway automatically activates another sensory pathway in the brain. One of the most common forms of synesthesia is grapheme–color synesthesia. This occurs when letters or numbers are associated with colors. Some synesthetes report that they actually see colors where letters appear, whereas others claim that the colors appear in their minds. The colors are usually consistent, meaning that for most synesthetes, As are consistently one color whereas Bs are consistently another color. Numbers are represented similarly, and can be reliably linked to a specific color. Other, less common, forms of synesthesia include sound–color and lexical–gustatory synesthesia. In sound–color synesthesia, sounds, or music, elicit colors. In lexical–gustatory synesthesia, words conjure tastes. Although synesthesia is a remarkable condition, it has received relatively little empirical attention until recently.

In the 1880s, Francis Galton was the first scientist to write about synesthesia. Unfortunately, few researchers studied it until the early part of the twentieth century. Two inventions appear to have contributed to the growing interest in synesthesia: the Internet, and noninvasive brain imaging techniques like functional magnetic resonance imaging (fMRI). Synesthesia is not listed in the Diagnostic and Statistical Manual for Mental Disorders because it alone rarely interferes with daily

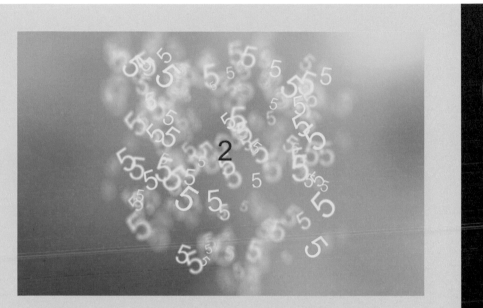

Figure 2.5 One common form of synesthesia is seeing a certain color in response to a specific letter or number. *(© Equinox Graphics/Photo Researchers, Inc.)*

functioning. Some people develop synesthesia as a result of drug use, stroke, or temporal lobe epilepsy. However, most lifetime synesthetes have never had any of these experiences. Their condition is at least partially hereditary and a function of neural development. Although people with synesthesia experience a difference in perceptual experiences, they do not perceive the condition as a handicap. To the contrary, many synesthetes view the experience as a gift, one that allows them unique artistic gifts or enhanced memory for words or numbers.

How or why synesthesia occurs is still unknown, although some neuroanatomical theories are emerging. Prevalence rates vary greatly. In 1880, Francis Galton argued that synesthesia

(continues)

(continued)

was as common as 1 in 20 people. Simon Baron-Cohen at Trinity College Cambridge estimates that synethesia affects approximately 1 in 2,000 people.[3] Vilayanur S. Ramachandran at the University of California–San Diego reports that his lab estimates that it is even more common—perhaps as many as 1 in every 200 people has synesthesia.[4] Recent research by Dr. Ramaschandran and his colleagues has provided instruments for identifying and testing synesthetes. His goal is to determine what neural processes cause synesthesia and underlie the phenomenon. The spectacular nature of the condition and its association with other conditions such as autism and temporal lobe epilepsy make it a hot topic for contemporary researchers.

(continued from page 27)

need some sort of guidelines to allow them to identify children and adults who have problems with autism so that they can help them learn how to function in a non-autistic world. Without a diagnosis, how will people with autism get the help and resources they need?

Though labeling theory tells us that a diagnosis can cause problems for someone with mental illness, there are benefits of the diagnostic process as well. Having a set of standards, a diagnostic category, helps clinicians and researchers design treatment for people with autism. Once researchers can identify a set of behaviors that cause problems for autistic people, they can figure out how to deal with those behaviors. Research essential to discovering the causes of autism and developing effective treatment for the condition requires the identification and participation of many people with similar problems. Practically, diagnosis makes it easier for people with autism to gain access to much needed treatment. The **Individualized Education Program (IEP)**, a product of the Individuals with Disabilities Act, assures that all children with mental or physical disabilities have the opportunity to have an education plan developed just for them. Without diagnosis that inevitably results from the identification of autistic behaviors, many children with autism would go without the special education they so desperately need.

• • • • • • • •

SUMMARY

Parents are usually the first to notice the signs of autism in their young children. Until the mid-twentieth century, autism was considered a form of childhood schizophrenia and was generally thought of as incurable. Early theorists blamed parents—particularly mothers—for their children's autistic behaviors. As the diagnosis of autism developed and took shape in the 1980s and 1990s, scholars worried about the effect of the diagnosis on young children. As a result, educators, therapists, and physicians use great care when identifying autism. Identifying autism allows a child access to special educational programs and essential treatment from an early age.

3

What Causes Autism?

Robert and Kristen have been married for 10 years. They live in the San Francisco area where both Robert and Kristen work as computer programmers for a software company. Both Robert and Kristen are quiet people; they are shy with others and usually prefer to be alone. They met on the job, and began a friendship when they discovered they shared a passion for the same video game. They live fairly predictable lives. They go to work and spend all their free time together on the computer or working in their garden.

When Robert and Kristen were in their late thirties, they decided that they wanted to have a child. When Kristen was pregnant, she was unusually cheerful and outgoing. She loved being pregnant, it made her feel like she was part magic; carrying a baby was a real gift. Sammy, an easy baby boy, was the perfect addition to their family. Kristen and Robert had never been so happy.

As Sammy grew, he was a quiet child. When Kristen took him to the park, she noticed how boisterous the other boys were. Sammy preferred playing with his trucks and digging in the sand to jumping or climbing on the play structures. Other parents commented on how peaceful Sammy was. Kristen was so proud of him. Their household was a quiet one and he fit in just fine. Sammy turned three in August and was scheduled to begin preschool a month later. Kristen approached choosing a preschool the way she approached a project at work. She researched every school within a 15-mile radius. She interviewed teachers, parents, and observed *classes. It was hard work for Kristen to talk to so many people, but she did it to ensure that her son could attend the best possible preschool. Ultimately, she settled on a Montessori school where the classroom was quiet, and children worked with materials that she thought would appeal to Sammy's organized nature.*

Kirsten stayed with Sammy in his classroom on his first day of school. He immediately found a sorting task that he enjoyed. It seemed that he acclimated perfectly. Within a few weeks, however, Sammy began to show some startling behaviors. He did love the sorting game, but he would not let any other child use it. When a teacher insisted that he share, Sammy could not be distracted and sat in the corner and rocked back and forth until he could return to sorting. The other children seemed to understand that Sammy was different. Sammy's teachers picked up on the tension between Sammy and his peers and tried to integrate him into the group. But Sammy was not interested in the other children. After three months, the teachers decided to talk to Kristen and Robert about Sammy's behavior.

When Kristen and Robert learned about Sammy's problems in preschool, they were not entirely surprised. In fact, Robert revealed that he had had similar problems as a child and had a special "social tutor" who came to his home to teach him how to look at and interact with other children. Kristen was always shy, and always felt disconnected from others. When Kristen, Robert and Sammy all met with a psychologist, they realized that they likely all lived with some form of autistic spectrum disorder. Though Kristen and Robert were content in their lives, they worried about Sammy. Would he suffer as a child and an adolescent as they did? Would he find a way to be productive as an adult? They were determined to help Sammy learn how to function in a non-autistic world, while not compromising his identity.

Parents of children with autism are faced with many pressing questions. "Why did my child develop autism?" "What causes the disorder?" "Is my child autistic because of something I did?" Researchers have been focusing on these questions for years. Although there is no single known cause of autism, biological, psychological, and social influences may contribute to the genesis, development, and maintenance of autism.

GENETICS

Genetics is the study of how characteristics are passed to us from our parents. Our genetic blueprint influences all human traits. **Deoxyribonucleic acid (DNA)** encodes genetic material into the nucleus of all human cells. Genes are the physical unit of heredity, formed from DNA and carried on **chromosomes**. Each human being has an estimated 30,000 separate genes that influence the development of all of his or her traits. **Geneticists**, people who study the way traits are passed on through heredity, are interested in determining just what genes are associated with a particular trait or behavior.

Human development and behavior is dynamic. The "nature versus nurture" debate refers to scientists and theorists discussing whether genes or environment predicts our behavior. In fact, the answer may be more complicated than previously thought. Our environment affects the expression of genes. For example, if most people in your family are tall, you may be predisposed to growing tall yourself. However, in the absence of a healthy diet, you might not grow as tall as your genes might predict. Your genes and your environment interact to produce a physical result: in this case, your height. Additionally, few human traits are determined by only one gene. Most behaviors, especially complicated sets of behaviors like those that result in autism, must be determined by the interaction of several genes. The **Autism Genome Project** originated in 2002, when researchers around the world decided to come together and share data in

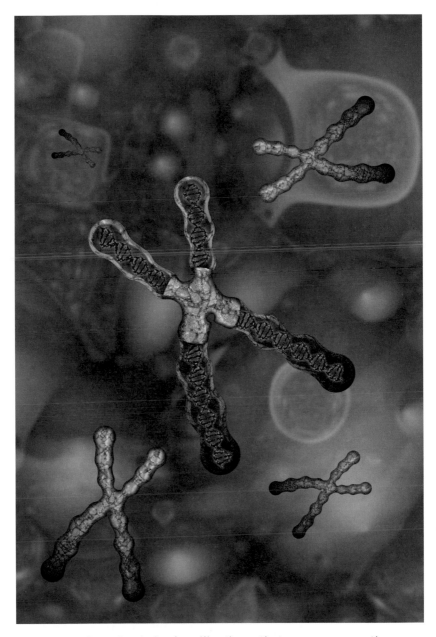

Figure 3.1 Complex behaviors like those that accompany autism result from the interaction of several genes. Genes are composed of DNA and carried on chromosomes. *(© Carol and Mike Werner/Visuals Unlimited, Inc.)*

order to find genetic similarities in autistic people from almost 1,200 families. Scientists in the project have identified five or six primary genes and as many as 30 **secondary** genes that they believe are involved in the development of autism. The goal of researchers in the Autism Genome Project is to identify autism "susceptibility genes." This means that they are looking for genes that increase the likelihood of autistic behavior. Further, autism susceptibility genes work together. This means that the more genetic markers for autism a person has, the more severe the autistic behaviors appear. The Autism Genome Project is still in its early phases and scientists will continue to focus on identifying patterns of genes that predict autistic behavior.

Recall that the prevalence of autism in the general population is approximately 1 percent. That means that out of every 100 babies born, approximately one will develop autism. However, for families with one autistic child, the risk that they will have another child with autism rises to 4 percent. Additionally there is a 4 to 6 percent risk that a sibling of an autistic child will have some sort of developmental problem or milder autism spectrum condition. That means that 10 percent of siblings of an autistic child have some autistic-spectrum condition. Due to the fact that autism is more prevalent in boys, brothers of autistic children have a higher risk (about 14 percent) of developing autism or some milder developmental condition.

One excellent way of determining the degree to which genes influence the development of a disorder is through a **twin study. Concordance rates,** or the degree to which both members of a twin pair have a specific condition, are the focus of twin studies. Twin studies compare concordance rates for **monozygotic twins** (MZ), or twins who share 100 percent of their genetic information, to the concordance rates for **dizygotic twins** (DZ) or twins who share 50 percent of their genetic material. If one MZ twin develops a disorder that is 100 percent hereditary, then his or her twin will develop it 100 percent of the time. Likewise, if a DZ twin develops a disorder that is 100 percent hereditary, there is a 50 percent chance that his or her twin will also have the disorder. Most psychiatric conditions are not 100 percent hereditary. Twin studies can help researchers determine the effect of genes on the development of a disorder like autism.

Anthony Bailey and his colleagues at the Institute of Psychiatry at King's College in London have been interested in genetic and cognitive markers of autism and autism spectrum disorders. In 1995, they concluded that about 60 percent of monozygotic twins are concordant for autism.[6] However, in about 90 percent of MZ twin pairs in which one twin has autism, the other twin has some cognitive or developmental problems that appear to be autism-related. Alternatively, Dr. Bailey and his colleagues found no dizygotic twins who were concordant for autism. The evidence from this study suggests that autism is strongly influenced by genes.

ENVIRONMENT

To date, scientists believe that there is no one path to autism. Instead, both genes and environment are implicated in its development. The **diathesis-stress model** holds that mental illness is caused by a genetic predisposition for a disorder accompanied by some environmental agent. For example, according to this model, someone with autism must have some autism genes and also be exposed to some toxic environmental event. An example of a toxic environmental event might include exposure to a virus while in utero, poisoning, or any severe trauma. Edwin Cook at the University of Chicago argues that prenatal environment may be key to the development of autism.[1] Birth complications that result from abnormal fetal development that is predetermined by genes might serve as the environmental agent that activates the genetic predisposition for autism. According to Dr. Cook, the dynamic interaction between genes and environment, beginning at conception, appear to lay the foundation for autism.

The road to autism can be divided into two paths: **idiopathic**, meaning the cause is unknown; and secondary, in which some abnormality—genetic or environmental—can be identified. Most people with autism are diagnosed with idiopathic autism whereas the remaining 15 percent have secondary autism. Known causes of secondary autism include exposure during pregnancy to German measles (rubella) and **thalidomide**. Thalidomide was a drug developed in the 1950s and prescribed to pregnant women worldwide to help ease the discomfort of morning sickness and to help induce restful sleep. Unfortunately, thalidomide caused thousands of babies to be born with severe deformities and developmental problems, including autism spectrum disorders. It is no longer used in pregnant women, and its use is strictly controlled. Though exposure to some environmental agents like German measles or thalidomide are known to cause autism in some children, it is unclear if those children who develop autism were genetically predisposed to the condition. Thus, German measles or thalidomide might serve as the environmental cause in the diathesis-stress model.

Childhood vaccines have been a topic of interest in the search for new environmental causes of autism. Parents and physicians became concerned about the use of vaccines after noticing that some children developed symptoms of autism after routine immunizations. Prior to 2001, mercury was used in a preservative in some vaccines. Both mercury and childhood immunizations have received a great deal of scientific scrutiny and no compelling evidence has emerged that associates vaccines with autism. Unfortunately, the myth of the association between vaccines and autism has gained such popularity in society that many parents refuse to vaccinate their children. According to the American Pediatric Association, the benefits of childhood immunizations far outweigh the risks.

Some promising recent research has focused on non-hereditary genetic markers in people with autism. A **mutation** is a permanent change in the DNA sequence of a gene. A mutation can be caused by miscopying during cell reproduction or it can be due to some environmental cause like exposure to radiation. A mutation by definition is a random event and usually has harmless consequences. However, some mutations can lead to disease. Dr. Jonathan Sebat and his col-

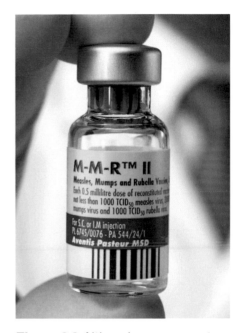

Figure 3.2 Although some parents and physicians were concerned about the appearance of autism after routine vaccinations, there is no compelling evidence that associates vaccines with autism, and the American Pediatric Association reports that the benefits of childhood immunizations far outweigh the risks. (© Saturn Stills/ PhotoResearchers, Inc.)

leagues at Cold Spring Harbor Laboratory in New York have discovered a form of autism that appears to be nonhereditary.[2] By evaluating the DNA sequences of autistic children and their parents, Sebat and colleagues identified similar mutations in several autistic children that were absent in their non-autistic parents. This means that some people with autism develop the disorder independent of family history. Dr. Kenny Yee of the

Cold Spring Harbor study believes that the incidence of the spontaneous (unpredictable) genetic mutations is due, at least in part, to increasing parental age. The findings of this study are compelling and point to a future in which we might have a genetic test for autism for unborn children.

SOCIOECONOMIC STATUS

Socioeconomic status, or one's social position, affects nearly all areas of one's life. For example, the neighborhood in which you live often determines which school you attend. Some schools are better than others, and most excellent schools are found in wealthier neighborhoods. Socioeconomic status can also affect health. Some people who live in low-income housing might be exposed to more airborne toxins, and thus be more likely to develop asthma or chronic bronchitis. Research consistently shows that many mental disorders appear to be elevated in people of low socioeconomic status.

There are two proposed explanations for why this might be the case. The **sociogenic hypothesis** holds that because living in poverty is more stressful, one's risk for developing a mental disorder is increased. One can imagine that relative to a mother with more resources, an impoverished pregnant woman is less likely to receive adequate prenatal care, is more likely to be exposed to viruses, and is more likely to experience a complicated delivery. Further, living in an impoverished condition can be more emotionally stressful than living a comparably privileged life. Stress can be the trigger that causes many mental disorders including schizophrenia, major depression, eating disorders, and anxiety disorders. Alternatively, the social drift hypothesis, also known as **downward drift,** suggests that people with mental disorders drift down the socioeconomic ladder because of their social and occupational impairment. So which is true? Research

Figure 3.3 Recent research identified nonhereditary genetic mutations—permanent changes in the DNA sequence of a gene—in several autistic children, indicating there may be a nonhereditary type
of autism. *(© Mopic/Shutterstock)*

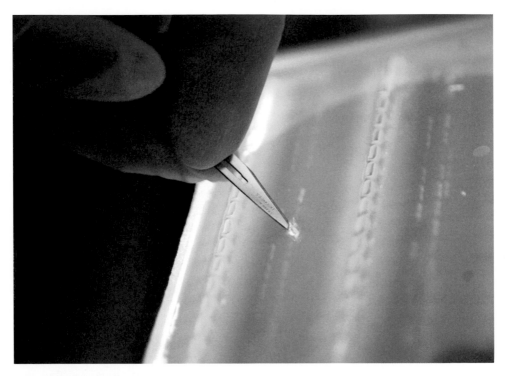

Figure 3.4 A researcher cuts a DNA fragment for DNA sequencing that will determine the presence of genetic mutation. This is how researchers at New York's Cold Spring Harbor Laboratory discovered a form of autism that appears to be caused by nonhereditary genetic mutation. *(© AP Images)*

shows that more cases of many mental disorders develop in families of lower socioeconomic status, but patients also drift downward because of their illness. Thus, both the sociogenic and the social drift hypotheses correctly predict many types of mental illness.

Autism is found at all socioeconomic levels. Leo Kanner, the scientist who first identified autism, argued that it was an illness that primarily affected the privileged. So far, this had not been confirmed. However, recent research suggests that autism is more likely to be identified in families at higher socioeconomic levels. Children from middle or upper class families are more likely to receive regular health care and be enrolled in preschool or child care in which they are exposed to professionals who are trained to identify signs of autism early. That means that these children are more likely to be diagnosed and treated before they even begin kindergarten. Impoverished children might not see a pediatrician regularly, nor will they begin school until they are five years old. That can prevent the early identification of autism and hinder the commencement of treatment. So far, autism appears to be an "equal opportunity" condition. However, early identification of the disorder clearly favors those who have access to excellent medical care and educational opportunities.

• • • • • • • •

SUMMARY

This chapter examined the causes of autism and how and why it develops. Autism has a significant genetic component. A parent with one autistic child has an elevated risk of having another child with autism. Additionally, children with autism are likely to have family members who show autistic characteristics like developmental or cognitive delays. Promising research from New York suggests that spontaneous mutations might account for the increasing prevalence of autism in families with no history of the disorder. Although historically parents were blamed for autism in their children, there is no evidence supporting the veracity of the "refrigerator mother" hypothesis. Environmental triggers that contribute to autism include primarily biological events including exposure to prenatal toxins and birth complications. Autism does not appear to discriminate based upon socioeconomic level, although

(*continues on page 47*)

Donna Williams, author of *Nobody, Nowhere*

In 1995, the fourth edition of the *Diagnostic and Statistical Manual for Mental Disorders (DSM-IV)* was published. In this edition, the autism diagnosis was broadened, and clinicians and researchers were beginning to view autism as a spectrum disorder. At this time, autism was gaining speed as a diagnosis of interest in the psychiatric community. Donna Williams, an Australian performance artist, poet, and musician, published her first autobiography, entitled *Nobody Nowhere*. She describes her book as a "stream of consciousness" account of growing up confused, alienated, and misunderstood as an undiagnosed autistic youth. Williams' book was the first autobiography of an autistic person, and helped shape our understanding of the internal world of autism.

Donna Williams was born in 1963, in Melbourne, Australia. As a two-year-old, she was diagnosed with psychosis due to her odd behavior. Her parents and physicians constantly tested her hearing, as they were convinced that she was deaf. Williams herself describes a childhood of abuse and chronic illness, due to her unexplainable food allergies, blood sugar irregularities, and immune problems. She was on antibiotics constantly and reports that she was sickly throughout her early years. She claims to have had to create new personalities to help her deal with her inability to understand other people. While she understood basic language, emotion and intention continued to elude her. Williams struggled with social interactions and used "Willie," an imaginary personality, to help her navigate her social world.

Unfortunately for Williams, she was not diagnosed with autism until she was in her twenties. According to Williams,

Figure 3.5 Donna Williams. *(Donna Flinders)*

she wrote *Nobody Nowhere* in four weeks and delivered it to a psychiatrist. It appears that her biography helped the psychiatrist determine that among other ailments, many of Donna's problems could be explained by autism. The book was published in the United Kingdom and quickly became a best seller. Although Donna considers herself primarily an artist, she is a frequent public speaker and educator on autism and has worked with hundreds of autistic people and their loved ones over the years.

Donna Williams has published four autobiographical books, four textbooks about autism, and one poetry and prose book. She also has written several screenplays, and at least one fictional novel. Her poetry helps to illustrate her struggle as

(continues)

(continued)

a misunderstood young child, and illuminates the isolation of autism. Below, you can read her poem, "Nobody, Nowhere."

Nobody, Nowhere

In a room without windows
In the company of shadows
You know they won't forget you
They'll take you in.

Emotionally shattered,
Don't ask if it mattered
Don't let that upset you
Just start again.

In a world under glass
You can watch the world pass
And nobody can touch you
You think you're safe.
But the wind can blow cold,
In the depths of your soul
Where you think nothing can hurt you,
Until it's too late.

Run till you drop,
Do you know how to stop?
The people walk right past you.
You wave goodbye.
And they all merely smiled,
For you looked like a child,

Never thought that they'd upset you,
They saw you cry.

In the war of your soul,
You can't hear them at all,
And the world becomes an echo
Of what's left outside.
But nobody can win,
If you can't let them in
And there's nobody to answer
From that place where you hide.

Take advice, don't question the experts.
Don't think twice, you just might listen.
Run and hide to the corners of your mind, alone,
Like a Nobody Nowhere.

© 1985 by Donna Williams, http://www.donnawilliams.net

(*continued from page 43*)

children from higher socioeconomic status families may be identified and subsequently treated for autism earlier than children from impoverished homes. In Chapter 4, you will read about treatment for autism, and learn how children and adults learn to cope with living in a neurotypical world.

Treatment of Autism: Intervention and Education

Charlie, a 14-year-old boy, has exhibited signs of autism since he was six months old. His mother recalls that he accidentally hit his head as an infant and afterward he quickly became socially aloof and isolated. After his fall, he spent a lot of time gazing at his hands while waving them in front of his face. He exhibited poor eye contact, and preferred isolated play until he was five years old. His physical development was normal, and as soon as he could run, he spent hours running in circles with an object in his hand. He engaged in a lot of stereotyped behavior including flapping his arms, jumping, and moving his hands in circles.

Charlie did not begin to speak until age four, and for a long time he primarily used single words. He often repeated phrases used by others, and echoed words and sounds. Charlie attended a special school for children with developmental disabilities until he was 11. Although Charlie was bright and could read, write, and was a talented artist, he exhibited a wide range of disruptive, repetitive behaviors. On one occasion, Charlie insisted that before lessons could begin, all of the students and his teacher must wear watches that he made. Charlie developed a wide variety of words and phrases and yet his speech remained devoted to his own interests. He tended to ask the same questions over and over and often made embarrassing comments about other people's appearance.

Charlie began to attend a regular public school at age 12. However, he continued to struggle interacting socially with his peers. Charlie much preferred the company of adults to kids his own age because he found it so difficult to understand the unwritten rules of adolescent social relationships. His sense of humor is immature, and he has difficulty understanding jokes. What Charlie lacks in social finesse he makes up for with his excellent memory. He is fascinated by maps and can draw them rapidly and accurately from memory. He is a good student and learns quickly and memorizes facts with ease. Charlie continues to work with a therapist and his educators to help him improve his social skills. Although Charlie is bright and methodical, without treatment, he will be limited by his inability to navigate his social world.

Fortunately for Charlie, his social difficulties were identified early. Charlie enrolled in a school that encouraged his strengths (his memory and intellect) while helping him to develop appropriate social behavior. When Charlie left the school at age 11, he was not cured, but he was able to function in a normal public school. Charlie benefited from an attentive mother and dedicated treatment and educational professionals to help him learn to manage his autism.[1]

No two children with autism are identical. Autism is heterogeneous, and each person who is affected by it is different. Similarly, treatment approaches differ depending upon the individual. There is no cure for autism. Instead, treatment approaches aim to help people manage disruptive behaviors and learn practical life skills. Many practitioners stress **early intervention**. Early intervention requires that autism be identified in a young child and an appropriate treatment strategy developed in a timely fashion. In this chapter, you will learn about a variety of treatment strategies used to help people with autism learn to live a healthy, productive life.

THE HISTORY OF AUTISM TREATMENT

Although autism has been part of the psychiatric nomenclature since the early 1900s, the perception of the condition, and

Figure 4.1 A speech pathologist interacts with a young girl diagnosed with autism. Early intervention is stressed by many practitioners since it allows for the development of an appropriate treatment strategy in a timely fashion. *(© AP Images)*

likewise its treatment, has changed dramatically over the past 100 years. Recall that until the 1960s, autism was linked with schizophrenia, and as a result, treatment was focused on containing the patient, rather than treating him or her. The earliest treatments for autism included electroconvulsive therapy (ECT), a process by which electrical current is administered to the brain. ECT is still used today, although its use is generally limited to people with treatment-resistant mood disorder. Another controversial treatment of autism was lysergic acid diethylamide, or LSD. LSD is a hallucinogenic drug, meaning it elicits sensory experiences in the absence of actual stimuli. Today, it is an illegal substance, used recreationally and pseudo-therapeutically. Although LSD has been banned from use as a therapeutic agent, a small group of individuals believe it can help people get in touch with their "actual" selves.

By the 1980s, behavioral treatments for autism were being widely used. Behavior therapy employs principles of **behaviorism** to encourage desired behaviors and extinguish unwanted behaviors. In the 1950s, B. F. Skinner, a psychologist at Harvard University, observed that we engage in many behaviors because we receive a reward, or reinforcement, after the behavior takes place. For example, your parents might give you your allowance after you have completed your chores. In this case, you do your chores in order to receive your reward: your allowance. However, we also engage in behaviors in order to avoid certain negative consequences. Consider going to the dentist. Most people would not choose to go to the dentist just for fun. However, if you do go to the dentist regularly, you may be able to avoid more invasive and painful dental procedures that result from tooth decay.

According to the theory of **operant conditioning**, the likelihood that you will engage in a behavior increases if the consequence of that behavior is positive. Reinforcement occurs when a behavior is followed by an event that makes you want to repeat the behavior (like getting your allowance after doing your chores). There are three possible outcomes of behavior that make it likely that you will do it again: **positive reinforcement**, **negative reinforcement**, and **punishment**. Positive reinforcement occurs when something good happens after a behavior. For example, if you tell a joke and people laugh, you are receiving positive reinforcement for telling that joke. You are more likely to tell the same joke (or the same kind of joke) again. Negative reinforcement occurs when you do something in order to avoid or to stop something unpleasant. An example of negative reinforcement is telling someone you are sorry because you feel guilty about something you have done. Once you apologize, you feel better. That makes you more likely to apologize when you have done something that has hurt someone's feelings. If a dog engages in an unwanted behavior (like a puppy taking food off the table), some people will squirt the dog with a water gun. This is an example of punishment—administration of an unpleasant stimulus with the intention of lowering the likelihood that the behavior will occur again.

In this section, you will learn about four approaches to treating children with autism. The severity of autism varies, and as such, traditional treatment models vary as well. The overall goals of treatment are shared by all treatment philosophies. **Behavior modification**—the eliminating of unwanted or dangerous behaviors and increasing prosocial positive behaviors—is perhaps the most important goal of autism treatment. Clinicians want their patients to improve their social skills so that those with autism can attain the highest quality of life possible. Traditional treatment methodologies for autism do not aim to cure the disorder. Autism, as it is presently understood by the scientific community cannot be cured, though its symptoms may be managed. However, alternative therapies currently being developed and tested outside of the traditional medical community do aim to cure autism, to help children completely recover from the disorder.

In considering the value of any treatment program, it is important to review all of the scientific information related to its efficacy. That is, are there published studies in peer-reviewed journals that support a particular treatment? Submitting a research article to a peer-reviewed journal ensures that the article will be evaluated by experts in the field to determine that the methodology is sound, the results are accurate, and the interpretations are appropriate. Some alternative or nontraditional treatments might claim tremendous success in treating or even curing children with autism, but may rely on anecdotal evidence.

Such practitioners might publish their own literature touting the success of their approach without submitting their studies to the scrutiny of other experts in the field. Consumers of services for the treatment of psychological disorders in general and autism in particular must be wary about the "scientific" information they might receive about a particular treatment program.

BEHAVIORAL APPROACHES

Applied behavior analysis is an approach to psychological treatment that is based upon the philosophy of B.F. Skinner. Skinner was a behaviorist, a psychologist who believed that only observable behavior—not thoughts or feelings—was worth scientific study. Recall that both genes and environment interact to produce behavior. Behavior analysts are most interested in how the environment causes changes in behavior. Conditions that have been the focus of behavior analysts include compulsive overeating, drug addiction, improvement of the workplace, as well as developmental disorders and juvenile delinquency. In the next section, you will read about Dr. Ivar Lovaas, who has modified traditional applied behavior analysis in order to develop a treatment specifically for children with autism.

One of the pioneers in autism treatment research is Ivar Lovaas at the University of California, Los Angeles. In the 1960s and 1970s, Dr. Lovaas began working with young children who showed significant speech delays and interpersonal problems. He developed an approach to treating autistic children based on the principles of applied behavior analysis. For more than 40 years, Dr. Lovaas has collected a huge amount of data supporting his approach and it is considered one of the most promising options for treatment of autism.

The Lovaas approach is suggested for children between the ages of two and eight. The institute recommends enrolling

Figure 4.2 One-on-one instruction is part of the treatment strategy developed by Dr. Ivar Lovaas, a pioneer in autism treatment research. *(© Brenda Carson/ Shutterstock)*

children as early as possible, ensuring that appropriate social behavior is taught at an early age. It is an intensive program, and children work one-on-one with a teacher for approximately eight hours a day, five to seven days a week. Compared to other treatments, the Lovaas approach is the most time-intensive. Lovaas and his colleagues emphasize family involvement so that what is learned in the classroom can easily translate into the home. Teachers begin with building positive interactions to encourage more initiation of social exchange. Using language is encouraged and rewarded. Early goals for young students include the development of new play skills, encouraging interactive relationships with others, and appropriate reaction to sensory input. An important focus for the Lovaas approach is on the development of cooperative play; a way of learning perspective-taking and understanding the give-and-take of social relationships.

Like most autism treatment programs, the Lovaas approach uses behavior modification. Again, behavior modification involves rewarding desired behaviors and punishing or ignoring negative ones. For example, teachers in the Lovaas school will reward positive behaviors, such as using language to ask for a toy, with a piece of candy. Lovaas practitioners rarely use punishment or the administration of an unpleasant stimulus in order to decrease the likelihood of an undesired behavior. Even then, punishment is reserved for children who demonstrated the most dangerous, self-injurious behaviors. Presently, the Lovaas method no longer includes physical punishment, instead relying upon negative reinforcement (taking away something desirable) and enthusiastic positive reinforcement for desirable behaviors.

The most striking aspect of the Lovaas approach is that it includes the most empirical evidence of its success. Many articles have been published in peer-reviewed journals and hundreds of children have been followed into their adult lives to track their progress. Dr. Lovaas has demonstrated extraordinary success in treating autistic children, and his methods have been well documented and examined thoroughly. There are now clinics using the Lovaas approach all over the United States and in the United Kingdom.

TEACCH

The Treatment and Education of Autistic and Related Communication-handicapped Children (TEACCH) was founded in 1966 by Eric Schopler at the University of North Carolina at Chapel Hill. It is a treatment approach designed to work within various real-world settings (e.g. public schools, family home, school bus) to help people with autism adjust to life in a "non-autistic" world. Schopler coined the term "culture of autism" to illustrate the kinds of difficulties people with autism face. According to Schopler, the culture of autism involves the following:

1. Relative strength in and preference for processing visual information (compared to difficulties with auditory processing, particularly of language)

The Curious Incident of the Dog in the Nighttime, by Mark Haddon

Published in 2003 by Vintage Books, *The Curious Incident of the Dog in the Nighttime* is not a memoir, nor is it autobiographical in any way. Instead, it is a novel, the story of a young autistic boy who decides to investigate the death of a neighborhood dog and eventually discovers a secret in his own family.

Mark Haddon, the author of the book, is a writer and teacher who worked with autistic children. The protagonist of his novel is Christopher John Francis Boone who shows some savant abilities coupled with the peculiarities of behavior and severe social impairment typical of autism. He knows the capitals of every country in the world and can name every prime number up to 7,057. Additionally, he will not eat foods that are touching, he detests anything that is yellow or brown, and he will scream or smash things when he is angry or confused. In the novel, Christopher spends a lot of time trying to understand why people do what they do and talking things over with his teacher, Siobhan. In this excerpt, Christopher is describing to a psychologist what makes a good day or a bad day:

2. Frequent attention to details but difficulty understanding the meaning of how those details fit together
3. Difficulty combining ideas
4. Difficulty organizing ideas, materials, and activities
5. Difficulties with attention—some individuals are very distractible, others have difficulty shifting attention when it's time to make transitions
6. Communication problems, which vary by developmental

> Mr. Jeavons, the psychologist at school, once asked me why four red cars in a row made it a Good Day, and three red cars in a row made it a Quite Good Day, and five red cars in a row made it a Super Good Day, and why four yellow cars in a row made it a Black Day, which is a day when I don't speak to anyone and sit on my own reading books and don't eat my lunch and take no risks. He said that I was clearly a very logical person, so he was surprised that I should think like this because it wasn't very logical.

Although Christopher can feel basic emotions, he has great difficulty figuring out what other people are feeling. Further, his own emotions, when more complicated than happiness or sadness, frustrate him to the point of having temper tantrums. Christopher's emotional responses are dictated by his autism. He forms easy bonds to routines and animals, whereas the human bond remains elusive. The story gives the reader real insight into the thoughts of an autistic boy and how confusing the outside world must be to someone like him.

Figure 4.3 Educators observe as an autistic student participates in an exercise employing the TEACCH method. TEACCH provides a structured environment for children with autism so that they can better understand what is happening around them and do things more independently. (© *AP Images*)

level, but always include impairments in the social use of language (called "pragmatics")

7. Difficulty with concepts of time, including moving too quickly or too slowly and having problems recognizing the beginning, middle, or end of an activity
8. Tendency to become attached to routines, with the result that activities may be difficult to generalize from the original learning situation and disruptions in routines can be upsetting, confusing, or uncomfortable

9. Very strong interests and impulses to engage in favored activities, with difficulties disengaging once engaged
10. Marked sensory preferences and dislikes[2]

Many of these descriptors likely sound familiar to you. What makes TEACCH unique is its intention to incorporate appropriate learning strategies into all areas of the autistic world. Visual stimuli are used in order to teach communication skills as well as illustrate the steps necessary to complete a complicated task. In order to inform people about the unique challenges of autism, TEACCH facilitators work with family members and educators to help design an "autism-friendly" environment in all areas of the real world. Treatment is designed for each child individually, depending upon his or her particular strengths and weaknesses. A structured environment, a predictable routine, and a reliance on visual learning helps people with autism gain self-confidence and a new skill set to help them live their lives.

JUDGE ROTENBERG CENTER

One controversial treatment program is the Judge Rotenberg Center located in Canton, Massachusetts. Matthew L. Israel, Ph.D., founded the center in 1966, when he began working with developmentally disabled children in a residential setting. Dr. Israel was a strict behaviorist, someone who believes that all behavior can be modified with the use of punishment and reward. A student of B.F. Skinner, Israel believed in applying Skinnerian models to the treatment of troubled children. The Judge Rotenberg Center now treats more than 200 students from all over the country. The center focuses on limiting or eliminating the use of psychotropic medication and applying behavior modification techniques in their place.

Figure 4.4 Matthew Israel, Ph.D., director and founder of the Judge Rotenberg Education Center. *(AP Images)*

The Judge Rotenberg Center has been controversial mainly for its use of "**aversives**" or physical punishments. The first types of aversives the center used included spraying misbehaving children with water, vapor (water mixed with pressurized air), or unpleasant tastes. Later, aversive treatment included the use of electric shock, via the application of a graduated electrical device (GED). Publicly, the philosophy of the center is that positive behaviors are generously rewarded and aversives are only used as a last resort. However, investigators from the New York State Board of Education found that there was insufficient monitoring of the administration of aversives, and concluded that they were being used on children or young adults who displayed little or no aggressive or self-injurious behavior. Although several attempts have been made by various courts to close the Judge Rotenberg Center, parents of disabled children consistently argue on behalf of the center and claim that the practices are successful in treating the most severely developmentally disabled children. At present, both a judge and the child's parents must approve the use of aversives before they may be added to the treatment plan.

The behavioral approach for the treatment of autism and related disorders is universal. Most popular and empirically grounded treatment programs employ some form of behavioral treatment. What becomes critical for parents—the usual consumers of these services—is that their children continue to be viewed as individuals. Although it seems easy to view behavior as it appears on the surface, revealing underlying causes of behavior can help clinicians and researchers understand the most appropriate methods of treatment.

PSYCHOPHARMACOLOGICAL TREATMENT

Most accepted treatment strategies for autistic people are behavioral or dependent upon social learning. For some people, autistic behaviors can be so severe or debilitating that prescription medication is used. Although rare, self-injurious behavior is a symptom of autism. When self-injury is difficult to control behaviorally, some psychiatrists will use antipsychotic medications or antidepressant medications in an attempt to minimize harmful behavior. According to the National Institute of Mental Health (NIMH), in 2006, the U.S. Food and Drug Administration (FDA) approved **risperidone** for the symptomatic treatment of irritability and the reduction of self-injurious behavior in autistic children and adolescents. Risperidone is an antipsychotic medication that is often used to treat schizophrenia. Antidepressant medications, more specifically the **selective serotonin reuptake inhibitors** (SSRIs) have been approved to treat some autistic children, beginning at age six. SSRIs have exhibited moderate success at reducing the repetitive, ritualistic behaviors associated with autism as well as increasing prosocial behaviors and decreasing social anxiety. This class of medication is very new, and its use in young children is not well understood. Though many types of SSRIs are FDA approved for use in children, parents and clinicians must monitor the administration closely.

Many children with autism have problems with sustained attention or focus. For them, the application of **Ritalin**, a drug commonly diagnosed for the treatment of attention-deficit hyperactivity disorder may be appropriate. According to

Figure 4.5 A teacher offers a reward to a student during a class at the Judge Rotenberg Educational Center in Canton, Massachusetts. *(© AP Images)*

treatment professionals, stimulants may actually help decrease impulsive behaviors that can be problematic in some people with autism. Finally, seizures—although rare—are more common in autistic people than in people without autism. When there is a risk of seizure, **anticonvulsant medications** are used. In addition to preventing seizure, many anticonvulsants work as mood-stabilizers. Anticonvulsants can be very effective, however their administration must be closely monitored. Blood levels are examined regularly in order to prevent an overdose of medication.

Physicians must use caution when prescribing any type of medication for use in young children. Not only are these medications new, we are learning more and more about the **plasticity**, or malleability, of the child's brain. So far, there is no way to predict what effect these medications will have on the developing brain. This uncertainty makes clinicians cautious in prescribing their use. Medications are usually considered a last resort, reserved for children who do not respond to psychological or behavioral methods of treatment.

DIETARY TREATMENT

Recently, media outlets have directed a great deal of attention to dietary treatment of autism and autism spectrum disorders. The dietary approach to autism is based on the idea that a food allergy, or a vitamin/mineral deficit is at the cause of some forms of autism. Considered "alternative treatments," some parents and clinicians report great success with eliminating foods from one's diet or prescribing vitamin or mineral supplements to people with autism. Although these treatments are now receiving more attention by scientists, so far we have little or no scientific data about the efficacy of such approaches. In order to determine the efficacy of a treatment, it must undergo clinical trials that would allow for comparison among the proposed treatment, established treatments, and no treatment. When such rigorous data emerges, we will surely have a more complete picture of the appropriateness of some of the dietary approaches to treating autism.

Although lacking in scientific support, some parents and clinicians advocate for a gluten-free, casein-free diet. Removing glutens and caseins from one's diet is challenging: Glutens are found in nearly all grains including wheat, oat, rye and barley; casein is a primary component of dairy products. Considering that the majority of many children's diets include glutens and milk, parents who decide to embark on this strict diet must be dedicated to its application. Anecdotal evidence for the gluten-free, casein-free diet is quite promising, although as previously mentioned, no rigorous studies exist yet to support its application. Supplements, such as vitamin B6, have been reported to be effective in reducing some of the asocial symptoms of autism. Finally, the use of **secretin**, a substance normally used for people with gastrointestinal problems, has been proposed as a possible treatment for autism. Although parent reports have suggested improvement in autism symptoms after secretin administration, there are no clinical reports supporting its efficacy.

ADDITIONAL THERAPIES

Sensory integration disorder and sensory integration therapy have recently become a hot topic among parents and educators. However, sensory integration disorder is not a condition recognized by the *Diagnostic and Statistical Manual of Mental Disorders.* As yet, there is little research regarding its existence, cause, or how to treat it. However, there are occupational therapists who claim to practice sensory integration therapy, and this can be persuasive to parents of children with autism. Although sensory issues are not a recognized symptom of autistic disorder or the autism spectrum, many people with autism do have difficulty processing certain sensory experiences. For example, some children with autism may have a preference for certain clothes because other clothes feel funny or uncomfortable on their bodies. This alone is not a sign of autism, as many young children can be incredibly particular about what they wear as they feel either constrained, restricted, or downright uncomfortable in certain clothing. Autistic people may become so overwhelmed by a sensory experience, such as a particular noise or feeling, that they engage in bizarre or seemingly meaningless behavior. When autistic children engage in repetitive behavior it is usually informative of some internal experience. Perhaps the child is having sensory difficulty, or is frustrated or anxious because of a particular experience. At any rate, aberrant sensory experiences are common to autism and as a result, some caregivers believe that treating the sensory problems can help eliminate other symptoms of the disorder.

Unfortunately, there is little data to support the use of sensory integration therapy in general, and with autistic people in particular. For that reason, parents are warned to investigate the credentials of anyone claiming to practice sensory integration therapy and to be forewarned that often such therapy is not covered by health insurance. Sensory integration disorder and its therapy are new ideas, and lack the rigorous scientific examination that more traditional conditions and therapies have endured. For now, we know very little about the condition and how best to treat it.

Although there is no known research investigating the efficacy of art therapy with autistic populations, some caregivers of people with autism believe that art therapy can help give their struggling family members a voice. Art therapy is used for all ages of people and is based on the idea that through accessing creative energy, one can express thoughts and feelings that may be consciously inaccessible. Autistic people are particularly impaired at understanding their feelings and the feelings of others. Art therapy, then, might help those with autism give a voice to those internal thoughts and feelings. The use of art therapy in the autistic community is new and its proponents call for rigorous scientific research to demonstrate its utility.

You read about Temple Grandin in the Sidebar for Chapter 3. Ms. Grandin is an outspoken autistic woman who has found refuge working with animal populations. Due to her insistence that animals can help autistic people connect with others, many people who work with autistic people believe that animal

(*continues on page 68*)

Jenny McCarthy

Actress Jenny McCarthy has received a great deal of attention in the press as the mother of an autistic child. Evan, born in 2002, began to experience seizures at the age of two-and-a-half. After several hospital visits, Evan was diagnosed with autism. In hindsight, McCarthy believes that she knew all along that something was different about Evan. Her mother-in-law had pointed out that he was not affectionate. Strangers had asked her questions about her son's odd behavior. Still, McCarthy ignored the signs until his physical health began to deteriorate.

When Evan received his diagnosis, McCarthy felt overwhelmed. A diagnosis of autism felt like a death sentence. She immediately began scouring the Internet looking for treatment options and recovery stories from other parents. One of her first attempts at healing Evan involved implementing a gluten- and casein-free diet. This meant eliminating all wheat and dairy products from Evan's meals. Thankfully, this approach appeared to help Evan, and, according to McCarthy, Evan noticeably improved his speech within two weeks. Noticing that Evan did not play with toys the way other children did, she began to help teach him how to "play." She showed him videos of children playing and used modeling techniques to help him learn to catch a ball. Play therapy coupled with the new eating habits appeared to help Evan—he was not cured, but his behavior was improving.

Like many couples with autistic children, McCarthy's marriage dissolved from the stress the diagnosis introduced into their relationship. Although both parents were invested in their son's prognosis, the emotional demands of raising an autistic son were intense. After the divorce, McCarthy felt alone and committed first and foremost to Evan. Although she wanted to become

Figure 4.6 Jenny McCarthy, Jim Carrey, and McCarthy's son, Evan Asher. (© AP Images)

involved in another relationship, she worried that her role as a mother with an autistic son would be off-putting to most men. That proved not to be the case. McCarthy began dating actor Jim Carrey, who is now prominently involved in the autism-awareness movement. In many of her interviews, McCarthy refers to Carrey as the "autism whisperer." Thus far, McCarthy has written two books for parents of autistic children, *Louder Than Words: A Mother's Journey in Healing Autism*, and *Mother Warriors: A Nation of Parents Healing Autism Against All Odds*. In many ways, McCarthy has given a voice to many frustrated and isolated parents struggling to raise autistic children.

As part of her journey to help her son Evan as well as increase autism awareness, Jenny McCarthy became involved with an

(continues)

(continued)

organization called Generation Rescue. Generation Rescue is an international organization involving parents, scientists, and doctors who are invested in discovering the causes of autism and developing successful treatments. Generation Rescue promotes a biomedical approach, meaning that its members believe that autism may be relieved by purging the body of toxins. Although there are several Web sites that offer ample anecdotal advice for this approach, so far, scientific-support is limited. Regardless, Jenny McCarthy and Generation Rescue have helped thousands of parents connect and feel like they have agency in their children's recovery.

(continued from page 65)

therapy can help their patients form emotional bonds that were previously unattainable. Dr. Ellen Langer of Harvard University demonstrated that elderly people who were given plants or pets to care for demonstrated less isolation and depression than elderly people who did not have plants or pets. Similarly, people with autism may benefit from the responsibility of caring for a creature that requires little emotional connection, but instead relies on the routines of feeding, walking, and play. Routines are often quite natural for people with autism; as a result caring for animals can be easy and a joy for autistic patients. Some experts believe that caring for animals can help people with autism develop relationships with others, feel less lonely and isolated, and help with their aggressive and frustrated feelings. Like art therapy, there is little if any research investigating the efficacy of animal therapy with people with autism. For now, it remains a marginal treatment approach used by several clinicians in addition to more traditional, prescribed therapies.

AUTISM AND THE FAMILY

The delay in diagnosis for someone with autism can put particular strain on a family. Although many children are identified before age three, other children may go for years without an accurate diagnosis. The frustration of not knowing what is wrong with one's child can lead to a tremendous amount of questioning, self-blame, and anger. It can be particularly challenging for some couples to remain committed to one another while raising an autistic child. According to the Autism Awareness Week data from the United Kingdom collected in 2003, autistic children were more likely to be raised in single-parent homes than dual-parent homes.[3]

Once a diagnosis is reached, family members may react in a variety of ways. They may cry, express frustration or anger, or even denial. They may seek several other clinicians looking for a second opinion. Alternatively, many family members may be relieved—relieved to finally have a name to put on the challenges that they are living with and relieved to learn that they are not to blame for the condition. As you learned in Chapter 3, contemporary theories regarding the causes of autism remove all responsibility from the parents. For parents who have been struggling with understanding a challenging child, news of the diagnosis of autism can be a relief.

Sometimes, we forget that autism is a developmental disorder that emerges in childhood but which continues into adulthood. Though there are several treatment approaches and facilities designed to help children with autism, adults with autism may be overlooked. Parents of adults with autism may have to deal with a particularly high level of stress. As their own parents age and require more of their children's attention, parents of autistic adults may find themselves worrying about caring for both their own parents as well as their children. The financial and time commitments necessary to care for multiple family members can prevent retirement, limit personal time, and challenge family relationships. Parents of adults with autism may need particular support in balancing the unusually complicated demands of caring for their families.

• • • • • • • •

SUMMARY

Treatment for autism has advanced significantly. Prior to the mid-twentieth century, autism was widely considered a form of childhood schizophrenia. Early treatment for autism included ECT and the administration of LSD. The early goals of autism treatment were not improvement of the condition, but rather to control the patient. Contemporary treatment approaches include behavior modification, educational programs, and family outreach services. Although there are little data to support alternative treatments including dietary modification, art therapy, or sensory integration therapy, research continues to help determine what other forms of treatment might be successful in improving the lives of those who live with autism. Having an autistic family member can be stressful for all family members. As a result, it is crucial to provide clinical services to family members struggling to live with and understand an autistic relative. Many researchers are actively working on developing more effective treatment approaches for autistic people and are committed to their evaluation using rigorous scientific standards.

Asperger Syndrome

Janet is a first-year graduate student in the computer studies department of an elite university. She is quiet and usually keeps to herself. Janet is attractive, but her anxiety in social situations limits her interactions with potential dating partners. As soon as one of her classmates notices her, he usually concludes that she wants nothing to do with him because of her off-putting behavior. In reality, Janet is incredibly shy and awkward around others. She knows that her unfailing ability to tell the truth makes people uncomfortable around her. Furthermore, she often has problems understanding metaphors, sarcasm, and humor. She would like to fit in with her peers, but finds their ways of interacting puzzling.

Janet was, by all accounts, a normal child. She had a few words by the time she was two, but she rarely used them unless she really needed something. The curious part of Janet's communication was that she could speak fluently with her stuffed toys; when expected to speak with adults or other children, she struggled to get a word out. Janet's parents recognized that she was bright from an early age. She obsessed about letters, and was able to read and spell by the age of three-and-a-half. From that point on, Janet immersed herself in books. Unlike most children, Janet was relatively unin-terested in stories. Instead, she liked to memorize words. She loved a wildlife guide book and would memorize examples from the animal kingdom with the correct terms for each category of the taxonomy. Kingdom, phylum, class, order, family, genus, species:

Janet could recite each category in order for hundreds of animals. Give her a family, she could name several corresponding genera, and even more species. Her parents were thrilled; they believed they had a genius in the family. What they did not understand was that although Janet had remarkable memorization skills, her problem-solving skills were behind those of her peers. Furthermore, she was so uncomfortable around her peers that she had few friends and trailed behind her classmates in terms of social development.

As Janet grew up, she struggled to fit into her peer group. She realized that she was different, and she could identify ways in which she stood apart from others. She really could not understand nonverbal behavior or anything that was at all nonliteral. This frustrated Janet, and she began working with a therapist who helped her memorize the rules of social convention. She learned how to carry on a conversation, she learned how to answer questions directly, and she tried to remember to look people in the eye. By the time she got to college she was able to interact with her peers relatively normally. Unfortunately, her discomfort remained and caused her to remove herself from most social situations.

Janet is now 23 and has never had a romantic partner. She believes she is heterosexual, but has never been on a date. Although she is often approached, she knows her behavior is off-putting. Many young men in her classes think she is a snob because of how cold she can be. The truth is, Janet is quite the opposite: She is warm and friendly once someone takes the time to get to know her. Though she is hard to get to know, Janet is a good friend. She wants to fit in, have friends, and go on dates, but she struggles in new situations.

Autism is a spectrum disorder, which means that the severity of the disorder varies along a continuum, with some people exhibiting severe symptoms and others showing only a few. Asperger syndrome, a condition often likened to a mild form of autism, shares many characteristics with autism. Social functioning is impaired, communication skills are atypical, and the ability for perspective-taking is limited. Someone with Asperger syndrome may show unusual interest in specific habits or activities, coupled with an intense ability for concentration. Unlike someone with autism, people with Asperger syndrome demonstrate no significant speech impairment and can be very bright. They may excel in fields in which their interaction with the outside world is limited. With **social skills training**, someone with Asperger syndrome may be able to excel in nearly any domain. Whereas autism can be very limiting for people, Asperger syndrome has a more promising prognosis and has actually been considered by some to be more of a personality type than a mental illness.

HISTORY OF THE ASPERGER DIAGNOSIS

Hans Asperger was an Austrian physician who was a contemporary of Leo Kanner, the physician credited with identifying autism. Compared to Kanner's patients, who were predicted to have a poor prognosis, Asperger's patients were more likely to find ways to succeed, at least occupationally. He identified a group of boys who were **egocentric** (generally self-focused), socially awkward, and physically clumsy. The boys had a difficult time making friends, although they demonstrated incredible focus and knowledge in particular subjects. In fact, Hans Asperger called his patients "little professors" due to their ability to hold one-sided conversations on their topics of interest.

A 2007 report by Viktoria Lyons and Michael Fitzgerald of Trinity College in Dublin, Ireland, suggests that Hans Asperger most likely demonstrated many of the traits he studied. Asperger was born to a farming family in Austria and according to biographical reports, demonstrated great talent in languages from an early age. Apparently, he frequently recited poetry by Franz Grillparzer, the Austrian national poet, often to uninterested audiences. As a child he had difficulty making friends, and was considered physically awkward. Over time, he developed his intellectual gifts and became an influential and prolific physician and writer.[1]

How might sharing the traits of the boys he studied affect Asperger's perception of his patients? Asperger was known for minimizing the difficulties of Asperger syndrome and focusing on the great intellectual talents in many of his patients. His own struggle with the disorder, coupled with his great focus and intellect, might have helped him to understand the promise of those with Asperger syndrome. Alternatively, some argue that because Asperger's early work took place during World War II, he may have been attempting to protect his patients from being sent to concentration camps. Although Asperger's motivations may never be understood, there is significant biographical information to suggest that his passionate work with children with Asperger syndrome may have been at least partially driven by a desire to understand himself.

WHO HAS ASPERGER SYNDROME?

Most studies investigating the prevalence of Asperger syndrome do not discriminate between Asperger syndrome and autism. This means that most prevalence estimates for autism include Asperger syndrome, and many estimates of the prevalence of Asperger syndrome include autism. A 2008 report published in the *Journal of Autism and Developmental Disorders* concludes that estimates of Asperger syndrome are approximately half that of autism. They observe that for every 10,000 children, between 8 and 9 will have Asperger syndrome.[2] As with autism, males are more likely than females to be diagnosed with Asperger syndrome. Curiously, the more low-functioning the autistic person, the more likely they are to be female. This means that although males far outweigh females in high-functioning Asperger syndrome, the ratio becomes smaller as the impairment becomes greater.

IQ, or **intelligence quotient**, is a number used to reflect one's performance on a series of tests. There are many situational variables that can affect one's IQ, like stress, mood, and socioeconomic status. The purpose of IQ measurement, particularly in research studies, is to identify differences between groups. If true differences in IQ exist between autism and Asperger syndrome, then perhaps that should be a diagnostic criterion. At present, having an IQ of less than 70 requires that someone who displays characteristics of autism or Asperger syndrome be diagnosed with autism. However, according to Patricia Howlin at St. Georges Hospital Medical School in London, England, there is no difference in IQ between people with autism and people with Asperger syndrome. People with Asperger syndrome who have higher IQs have better social skills and interpersonal functioning than people with autism with a similar IQ. This suggests that IQ is not an appropriate criterion for diagnosis of autism spectrum disorders. Instead, IQ might help clinicians determine the kind of treatment that is most appropriate and help loved ones anticipate the patient's needs in the future.

TREATMENT OF ASPERGER SYNDROME
Although many of the symptoms or signs of Asperger syndrome cannot be cured, physicians, psychologists, and educators can develop a plan to help someone identify behavioral problems and change them effectively. According to the Mayo Clinic, treatment for Asperger syndrome typically has three components: communication and social skills training, **cognitive behavioral therapy**, and, occasionally, medication.

Social Skills Training

As with autism, people with Asperger syndrome have a fundamental problem interacting with people. Janet, the subject of the case study at the beginning of the chapter, most likely received social-skills training as part of her therapy as a child. Social skills training can help children and adults with Asperger syndrome learn how to process and participate in

John Robison

There are few first-person accounts of Asperger syndrome. John Robison is the author of a memoir about his life as an "Aspergian,"—from his days as a child with a condition that was largely unrecognized, to a successful career as an auto mechanic and author. In *Look Me in the Eye*, Robison describes what it means to live with a condition that makes social interactions utterly puzzling. Robison was not formally diagnosed with Asperger syndrome until he was in his forties. As a child, he struggled to fit in with his peers. Though he was very bright with an affinity for mathematics and science, he dropped out of school in the tenth grade. Largely self-taught, Robison managed to live a successful, productive life in a variety of careers including working as a sound engineer for the rock band Kiss, an executive for a toy company, and finally, the owner and manager of a highly successful auto-repair shop for luxury cars. His memoir details his problems deciphering social relationships as well as his unique understanding and use of language. Below is an excerpt from his book that details his preference for working with machines, rather than people:

everyday social interactions. In much the same way young students learning a new language and culture must study the subtle signs of communication, someone with Asperger syndrome will be explicitly taught the unspoken rules of social interaction. People like Janet can learn to answer questions directly and look people in the eye. Over time, and preferably with early intervention, someone with Asperger syndrome

Many people with Asperger's have an affinity for machines. Sometimes I think I can relate better to a good machine than any kind of person. I've thought about why that is, and I've come up with a few ideas. One thought is that I control the machines. We don't interact as equals. No matter how big the machine, I am in charge. Machines don't talk back. They are predictable. They don't trick me, and they're never mean.

I have a lot of trouble reading other people. I am not very good at looking at people and knowing whether they like me, or they're mad, or they're just waiting for me to say something. I don't have problems like that with machines.

Robison is married and has one child. He lives in western Massachusetts, where he spent much of his youth. His business, J.E. Robison Service Company, repairs and restores fine cars. He speaks frequently about Asperger syndrome to clinicians, educators and laypeople in order to increase understanding and appreciation for the unusual condition with which he lives.

Figure 5.1 Children with Asperger syndrome participate in a theater therapy program designed to help them practice social skills in a safe atmosphere. *(© AP Images)*

can become more skilled (and more comfortable) in everyday social situations.

Cognitive Behavioral Therapy (CBT)

Many people with Asperger syndrome have an intense interest in one or two topics. This obsession can be quite intense, and any interruption may lead to an angry outburst, or, at the very least, confusion. We all become frustrated occasionally. Sometimes, particularly for young children, it is very difficult to control negative emotions, which may lead to tantrums. Over time, people without a psychological disorder learn to deal with their frustration appropriately. Inhibiting anger or finding an appropriate coping strategy can pose a real challenge for someone with Asperger syndrome. One reason that people with Asperger syndrome become frustrated easily may be because they struggle to understand their own feelings as well as those of other people. Recall that Janet experiences anxiety in social situations. As a young girl, Janet may have struggled to understand her avoidance of her peers. Without the vocabulary and ability to understand her feelings, Janet would have felt even more isolated. Treatment with CBT can give someone with Asperger syndrome the tools to identify emotions, recognize behaviors, and develop coping strategies that are appropriate to the situation.

Medication

Medication is very rarely used to treat people with Asperger syndrome. No medication has been developed or determined to "cure" the problems associated with the condition. When medications are prescribed, they are usually intended to help one manage repetitive behaviors or mood problems that are inhibiting social growth and interfering with treatment progress. Some people with Asperger syndrome suffer from debilitating anxiety in social situations. This anxiety may be learned—that is, negative social interactions might lead someone to avoid future social situations. When confronted with a social situation, someone with Asperger syndrome may be extremely fearful or nervous—so nervous, in fact, that he or she is unable to enter the situation at all. Antianxiety medication may then be administered to help people with Asperger syndrome relax and practice new situations without the burden of extreme anxiety and the physical symptoms that accompany it.

Although rare, the intense focus of some people with Asperger syndrome may cause intrusive obsessive thoughts that significantly impair their functioning. When repetitive

Figure 5.2 Mainstreaming is the enrolling of children with disabilities, such as Asperger syndrome, in schools with nondisabled children. (© Matka_Wariatka/ Shutterstock)

behaviors become so severe that someone has difficulty controlling them or the person becomes aggressive when interrupted, antidepressant medications may be prescribed. The goal of medication in this case is to make life less stressful, emotions more manageable, and social situations less frightening.

Education
People with Asperger syndrome are typically of normal to high intelligence. **Mainstreaming**, or enrolling children with disabilities with nondisabled children is often the preferred course of education. All students have the right to public education. For this reason, children with disabilities and their families may

choose to work with an educator to create an Individualized Education Program (IEP). For a child with Asperger syndrome, academic accommodations might be unnecessary. However, special social tutors might be recruited to help students learn appropriate classroom behavior. Many people with Asperger syndrome are excellent students and may attend elite universities. Like Janet, people with Asperger syndrome often have tremendous focus and memory skills that help them excel in school. Often, the most challenging part of school for someone with Asperger syndrome are social situations. In order to cope with those challenges, educators often incorporate a social skills training component into the classroom to help their students reach their full potential.

• • • • • • • •

SUMMARY

Asperger syndrome is often considered to be a mild form of autism. Compared to autistic children who show a significant speech delay, children with Asperger syndrome begin to speak at a time that is developmentally appropriate. Intense interest in a few obscure topics is common in people with Asperger syndrome. When this interest is coupled with higher than average intelligence, people with Asperger syndrome can excel in many fields. Social skills are significantly impaired in Asperger syndrome, and treatment options are intended to help individuals manage interpersonal situations and relationships. Medication is used primarily to help patients cope with negative emotions like anxiety or depression or manage repetitive behaviors.

6 The Debate: Is There an Epidemic?

Jordan is a bright-eyed, five-year-old boy who loves fire trucks.
He has a vast collection of fire trucks, and his room is filled with
fire truck–themed décor. Unfortunately, Jordan is nearly mute. He
has three words: "drink," "cheese," and "truck." His parents are
devastated. Jordan is their only child and they fear that he will live
his entire life in an institution.

Jordan's parents, Bill and Tanya, have sacrificed their careers
and their relationship to find a cure for their son. Bill, a lawyer,
left his firm and works part time from home to take care of Jordan.
Tanya, a bookkeeper, also works part time so that she can be at
home with Jordan the other half of the time. They no longer are
willing to leave Jordan with a caregiver. Though they have tried
several, all have either proved incapable of handling Jordan's
tantrums and peculiarities or they have quit—most likely out
of frustration. Although Jordan should be in school and would
qualify for special education programs, he cannot enroll because
Bill and Tanya refuse to get the vaccinations required of all school-
children in his district. In fact, Jordan would have qualified for
early intervention programs had he been on any vaccine schedule!
Unfortunately, his parents are convinced that the vaccinations
Jordan received as an infant caused his autism. The decision to not
complete Jordan's childhood vaccinations has limited his access to
all treatment programs that are publicly funded, and thus would
be provided to Jordan free of charge.

Bill and Tanya are resolved to being available to Jordan 24 hours a day. The strain on their relationship is palpable. They have not had an hour alone since Jordan was two, which is when his behavior became more difficult to manage. They seem to have nothing to talk about other than Jordan and his treatment, and they often fight over the next step to take. Any outsider would notice that Bill and Tanya are suffering as much as their son. They need help, both financial and personal.

Recently, Tanya has become interested in chelation therapy. Chelation therapy involves removing heavy metals from the body, a process that is not well understood. All she knows about the process are the success stories; Tanya has not heard anything negative about the process. Though the supplements are not covered by medical insurance and are expensive, Tanya insists she wants to try. She concludes that she has nothing to lose by trying. She has an appointment with a clinic that is a two-hour drive from their home. Tanya is determined to take Jordan and see what the doctors can tell her. After that she will go back to the behavior therapy. Somehow she will find the money for a personal tutor for Jordan. Maybe the combination of the two will finally result in some visible improvement in Jordan's behavior.

Childhood illness, whether it is physical or psychological, often receives a great deal of attention. Society is protective of its youth, and no one wants to see a child suffer unnecessarily. Additionally, parents can be a strong advocacy group—motivated by the desire to help their child, they will search relentlessly for explanations and treatment. Parents of autistic children have become particularly vocal in their struggle to understand what is happening to their child and how to "cure" them. There are costs and benefits of parents' passions. On the positive side, parents working together can raise money, direct funds into research and treatment, and provide education and support for each other in difficult times. Alternatively, parents can also become desperate consumers of any information that might point toward a cure, no matter how unlikely or how unfounded in science that information is. Autism is an area in which parents are both the leaders of the movement toward eradicating the condition, and the unfortunate victims of pseudoscience and misinformation.

WHAT IS AN EPIDEMIC?

Bill and Tanya's story is not unique. Autism puts enormous stress on a family, as caregivers struggle to find treatment for their child. All family resources may be drained: financial, marital, and personal. Hope, what parents cannot sacrifice, motivates them to try new things, and keep looking for answers.

The Internet has vastly changed the way we think about medical conditions. With the click of a mouse, we can find diagnoses, examples, theories, and treatment options for nearly any illness. The power this gives us as consumers is tremendous. We can go into a doctor's office as a participant in our treatment, rather than as a naïve consumer. However, because information on the Internet is largely unedited, it may also gives us access to misinformation, or information that is at the very least, one-sided.

Many believe that there is presently an "epidemic" of autism. An epidemic occurs when rates of a disease occur in the human population at a rate greater than would be expected during a limited period of time. Many outspoken celebrities including NFL quarterback Doug Flutie and actress Jenny McCarthy argue that autism rates are increasing at epidemic proportions. The claim that autism is on the rise is usually accompanied by a request for more money to invest in its research and treatment. Although most prevalence studies do indicate that more children are being diagnosed with autism now than at any time previously, there are many reasons why we should not assume that there is an epidemic of autism.

DIAGNOSTIC CHANGES

In 1980, the American Psychiatric Association published the third edition of the *Diagnostic and Statistical Manual of Mental Disorders, DSM-III*. By this time, researchers and clinicians became especially interested in identifying and classifying children who exhibited unusual, harmful, or maladaptive behaviors. *DSM-III* included a diagnosis of childhood autism, and that diagnosis changed yet again in subsequent editions published in 1987 and 1994. With each publication, the diagnostic criteria for autism broadened. The implications of these changes were two-fold: (1) all the children who were diagnosed with autism previously would still be diagnosed with the new editions; and (2) with each revision, as the criteria became more inclusive, even more children could be diagnosed with autism. Thus, regardless of whether there is a true change in the incidence of autism, at least since 1980, there has been an increase in its identification simply due to the broadening diagnostic criteria.

Leo Kanner officially identified autism as a condition in 1943. This does not mean that autism did not exist previously. Earlier physicians, including Sigmund Freud, recognized and reported autistic symptoms in their patients. However, interest in a condition waxes and wanes. This means that during one period in history people might be extremely interested in schizophrenia, and during another time depression might be a big focus of researchers. When our attention as clinicians, parents, educators, and researchers is directed toward a specific syndrome, it is likely that we are going to be primed to identify and attend to its cases. In autism research prior to 1980, prevalence studies used primitive methods of gathering data like going over hospital admission records in order to determine how common the disorder is. Now that autism is of great interest, researchers are actively looking for

Toni Braxton
Mother of an autistic son and spokesperson for Autism Speaks

Toni Braxton, the mother of two, is the recipient of six Grammy awards and has sold millions of albums worldwide. In 2006, her life changed when her youngest son was diagnosed with autism. Braxton had observed that Diezel was developing differently from his older brother, but had assumed that he would catch up over time; after all, each child is different. When Braxton was asked to remove three-year-old Diezel from his private school in Las Vegas and was referred to a treatment clinic, she was shocked to learn that what she thought were normal delays were symptoms of autism.

Diezel showed typical signs of autism, including repetitive movements and insistence on routine. He always wanted to sit on the left of people, and insisted on eating with the same fork and plate at every meal. His speech was significantly delayed and he had real problems socializing with others and making eye contact. Braxton dedicated herself to learning as much as she could about the disorder, getting the best treatment for her son, and becoming an advocate for parents of children with autism.

"I became determined to join Autism Speaks in its battle against this devastating disorder when autism became a part of my family's reality," said Braxton. "Autism Speaks is making remarkable strides on so many fronts, from dramatically cases. That means that they are advertising for studies to the public, to clinics, and to public schools to help gain access to cases to help us understand more about the condition. If more

increasing awareness about autism to effectively fighting for more government resources for families and researchers. I feel privileged to have the opportunity to help advance this cause in any way I possibly can."[1]

Autism Speaks is a non-profit organization dedicated to raising awareness and directing money into autism research. Bob and Suzanne Wright, grandparents of a child with autism, founded Autism Speaks in 2005. Bob Wright served as chief executive officer of NBC for more than 20 years. Autism Speaks has merged with both the National Alliance for Autism Research (NAAR) and Cure Autism Now (CAN), bringing together the nation's three leading autism advocacy organizations.

Figure 6.1 Tony Braxton is a spokesperson for Autism Speaks and the mother of a son with autism, Diezel *(right)*. (© AP Images)

people are looking for people with autism than were in 1980, it is likely that more cases are going to be identified.

POLICY CHANGES

Another historical event that may help explain the seemingly rapid rise in the incidence of autism was the 1975 passing of the Individuals with Disabilities Education Act (IDEA). IDEA is a civil-rights act that ensures that all children with disabilities have access to public education through the age of 21. Prior to the passing of IDEA, children with disabilities like blindness or deafness were excluded from public schools. Thanks to IDEA, children with diagnosed physical and psychological conditions are provided access to public schools. The benefits of IDEA are clear. All children should be provided access to a free education. However, the availability of special advantages in any form can motivate parents and educators to diagnose a child with a condition simply to obtain access to the Individual Education Plan (IEP). Though most children who gain access to special education need that treatment, many may be misdiagnosed as autistic simply because they have special needs that do not fall into an existing category. Autism has become a trendy diagnosis, and, like attention deficit disorder, may be an easy one to stretch in order to grant access to troubled children who need treatment of some kind but who do not cleanly fall into a diagnostic category.

IMPLICATIONS FOR HEALTH INSURANCE

Finally, the complexities of our health insurance system may contribute to the increased diagnosis of autism. Clinicians working with children who have psychological or behavioral problems need to be reimbursed. Some health insurance companies will limit their reimbursement policies to certain conditions. Alternatively, some diagnoses might allow a patient access to more hours of reimbursed treatment than others. In order to make the most of the dollars paid by an insurance company, clinicians might choose to diagnose a disorder that will allow the greatest reimbursement. Because the autism spectrum has become so broad, it is now easier to apply to children for insurance purposes. The motivation of most clinicians is not sinister or selfish; most clinicians want their patients who need help to have access to as much treatment as possible. Because treatment for mental disorders can be costly, making the most of one's health insurance benefits is essential for the best access to clinical services.

RESEARCH UPDATE

Autism receives a great deal of attention today. You will likely see stories in the newspaper, on television, or hear about it through your friends and families. After reading this book you might be more likely to pay attention to stories about autism in the media. People are especially interested in conditions that affect children. Research into the disorder will continue until we have a more complete picture of what autism is, what causes it, and what we can do to treat it.

According to Dr. Richard Deth, a microbiologist at Northeastern University in Boston, Massachusetts, research into the genetics and cellular functioning of autistic individuals is one area that offers promising information.[2] He and his colleagues believe that children with autism may have a special sensitivity to toxins in the environment, leading to a stress response in their cells. By indentifying differences in the cellular functioning of autistic children, specialized treatment programs might be developed. Perhaps there are biological differences that can be revealed to help us understand why boys are so much more likely to be affected by autism than girls. Maybe there is some genetic marker to identify who will develop autism. Gene therapies might be developed to help us "knock out" the genes that are active in the expression of autism.

Though we know that behavior therapy can be very effective in treating people with autism, its effectiveness varies across children. There is always room for improvement in the treatment of psychological disorders. Whether it is vitamin supplements, medication, therapy, or educational models, improving upon current treatment strategies is a worthwhile goal.

From a public health perspective, science-based education about autism is essential. Eradicating the myths and misinformation about the disorder will help parents focus on established, valid treatment programs in order to help their children. Further, as parents are such a motivated and powerful advocacy group, they ought to be armed with the latest research about the disorder. At a time when access to research funding is at a premium, hypothesis-driven work with an eye to improving the lives of those who are affected by autism is crucial.

● ● ● ● ● ● ● ●

SUMMARY

It is unlikely that there is an epidemic of autism. Several factors may increase the likelihood that more cases of autism are being identified. To begin, broadening of the diagnostic criteria certainly accounts for some proportion of the increase. New interest in the condition has changed the way researchers look for new cases of the disorder, which undoubtedly will lead to greater identification. The passing of the Individuals with Disabilities Education Act has motivated educators and parents to diagnose children in order to gain access to public funds for treatment for their students and children. Finally, limitations of our health insurance system might motivate clinicians to diagnose autism spectrum disorders in children in order to maximize insurance benefits to allow for more treatment access.

Chapter 1

1. Wisconsin Medical Society, "Savant Syndrome: Islands of Genius," http://www.wisconsinmedicalsociety.org/savant_syndrome (accessed May 20, 2009).

Chapter 2

1. A. Ashley-Koch et al., "Genetic Studies of Autistic Disorder and Chromosome 7," *Genomics* 61, 3 (1999): 227–236.
2. Temple Grandin, *Emergence: Labeled Autistic* (New York: Warner Books,1996), 38.
3. S. Baron-Cohen, L. Burt, F. Smith-Laittan, J. Harrison, and P. Bolton. "Synaesthesia: Prevalence and Familiarity," *Perception* 25, no. 9 (1996): 1073–1080.
4. V.S. Ramachandran, and E. M. Hubbard. "Synaesthesia: A Window Into Perception, Thought and Language," *Journal of Consciousness Studies* 8 (2001): 3–34.

Chapter 3

1. A. Bailey, A. Le Couteur, P. Gottesman, P. Bolton, E. Simonoff, E.Yuzda, and M. Rutter, "Autism As a Strongly Genetic Disorder: Evidence from a British Twin Study," *Psychological Medicine* 25 no. 1 (1995): 63–77.
2. E.H. Cook, "Genetics of autism," *Mental Retardation and Developmental Disabilities Research Reviews,* 4 (1998): 113–120.
3. J. Sebat et al., "Strong Association of De Novo Copy Number Mutations with Autism," *Science* 316, no. 5823 (2007): 445–449.

Chapter 4

1. *Adapted from* Robert L. Spitzer, et al, *DSM-IV-TR Casebook: A Learning Companion to the Diagnostic and Statistical Manual of Mental Disorders, Fourth Edition,* (Washington, DC: American Psychiatric Pub, 2002), 355–356.
2. TEACCH.com http://www.teacch.com. [full citation TK from AU]
3. Steve Broach, *Autism: Rights in Reality: How People with Autism Spectrum Disorders and Their Families Are Still Missing Out on Their Rights.* (London: National Autistic Society, 2003).

Chapter 5

1. V. Lyons and M. Fitzgerald, "Did Hans Asperger (1906–1980) have Asperger's?" *Journal of Autism and Developmental Disorders* 37 (2007): 2020–2021.
2. Andrea Witwer and Luc Lecavalier, "Article name TK," *Journal of Autism and Developmental Disorders* (2008).

Chapter 6

1. Autism Speaks, "Toni Braxton Named National Celebrity Spokesperson for Autism Speaks," Autismspeaks.org, http://www.autismspeaks.org/press/braxton_spokesperson.php (accessed May 20, 2009).
2. Richard Deth, personal communication, February 6, 2009.

GLOSSARY

anticonvulsant medication—Medication intended for people with epilepsy, which can be effective in people with mood disorders and autism spectrum disorders.

applied behavior analysis—A treatment approach for autistic people that involves using learning principles to shape social behavior.

Asperger syndrome—A disorder on the autism spectrum, often considered high functioning autism.

Autism Genome Project—An international group of researchers who joined together in 2002 to focus on identifying the genes responsible for autism.

aversives—Unpleasant stimuli, such as electric shock, used by the Judge Rotenberg Center in the treatment of autism.

behavior modification—Changing behavior by rewarding positive behaviors and ignoring or punishing negative behaviors.

behaviorism—A psychological approach, prevalent in the 1930s through the 1960s, in which behavior, rather than thoughts or feelings, was the focus of scientific study.

chromosomes—The structures that carry genes, the building blocks of all living things.

cognitive behavioral therapy—Treatment approach in which both maladaptive thoughts and behaviors are identified and strategies for changing them are designed.

concordance rates—Used in twin studies, estimates of how often both twins develop the same condition.

continuum—A progression from one extreme to another.

diathesis-stress model—A model used to explain the etiology of psychological disorders that includes a combination of genetic predisposition and environmental stress.

disorders first identified in childhood—The category of psychological disorders in which autism is found in the Diagnostic and Statistical Manual of Mental Disorders. Also called pervasive developmental disorders.

dizygotic twins—Twins who come from two different eggs fertilized by two different sperm and thus share 50 precent of their DNA. Also called fraternal twins.

DNA (deoxyribonucleic acid)—The building blocks of our genes.

downward drift—The hypothesis that people with psychological disorders are more likely to be part of lower socioeconomic groups because their disorder limits their ability to succeed.

early intervention—A term used to describe treatment applied at the earliest sign of disorder.

egocentric—Self-focused.

electro-convulsive treatment (ECT)—A therapeutic approach in which an electric current is run across the brain, inducing seizures.

emotional reciprocity—The ability to understand how others feel and respond appropriately.

epidemic—A term used to define when cases of a condition appear at a rate that exceeds what would be expected.

etiology—The origin of a psychological disorder.

false-belief task—An experimental task used by clinicians and researchers to determine the presence of a theory of mind.

functional magnetic resonance imaging (fMRI)—A noninvasive way to observe brain structure and function.

Fragile X syndrome—The most common cause of inherited mental impairment.

gene—The physical unit of heredity, formed from DNA and carried on chromosomes.

geneticists—People who study how disorders are passed on from one generation to the next.

genetics—The study of genes and how they influence behavior.

hallucinations—A psychotic symptom in which someone has a physical experience in the absence of a stimulus, like hearing voices.

heredity—An estimate of the genetic contribution to the etiology of a condition. For example, the likelihood that parents with autism will have children with autism.

heterogeneous—Varied.

high-functioning autism—A term sometimes used to describe Asperger syndrome.

idiopathic—Of unknown cause.

Individualized Education Program (IEP)—A written educational plan to ensure that someone with special needs receives appropriate accommodations.

IQ (intelligence quotient)—A numerical estimate of intelligence based upon test performance.

labeling theory—The idea that the act of assigning someone a diagnosis, or label, increases the likelihood that he or she will behave in ways consistent with the label.

LSD (lysergic acid diethylamide)—A hallucinogenic drug previously used to treat autism.

mainstreaming—The act of putting children with psychological disorders into classrooms with nondisordered children.

milieu therapy—A therapeutic approach designed by Bruno Bettleheim in which patients are treated in a supportive, work and goal focused environment. Was previously used with autistic patients.

monozygotic twins—Also called identical twins. Twins who come from one egg fertilized by one sperm and share 100% of their genes.

mutation—A random change in the sequence of one's genes.

negative reinforcement—Increasing the likelihood of a behavior by removing an unpleasant stimulus.

neurotypical—A term used by many in the autistic community to describe people who do not have autism spectrum disorders.

operant conditioning—The theory that reinforcements, like reward and punishment can be used to increase or decrease the likelihood of a behavior.

pervasive developmental disorders—A category of disorders in the DSM-IV that includes autism and Asperger syndrome.

plasticity—A term used to describe the ability of the brain to change.

positive reinforcement—A positive event used to increase the likelihood of a behavior.

punishment—A negative event used to decrease the likelihood of a behavior.

risperidone—An anti-psychotic medication, usually used in patients with schizophrenia, which is also occasionally used to treat people with autism.

Ritalin—The psychiatric drug methylphenidate, generally used to treat attention deficit disorder, which is occasionally used to treat people with autism spectrum conditions.

savant—Someone with great intellectual abilities in a narrow area.

secondary—Used to describe people who develop autism from unknown sources. Describes the majority of people with autism spectrum disorders.

secretin—A substance normally used for people with gastrointestinal problems has been proposed as a possible treatment for autism.

selective serotonin reuptake inhibitors (SSRIs)—Antidepressant medications that are occasionally used to treat autism spectrum disorders.

sensation-seeking behavior—A trait that involves seeking out thrilling, or exciting situations.

social skills training—A treatment approach used for people with many different types of psychological disorders in which one learns independent living and interpersonal skills.

socioeconomic status—A descriptor for one's social, economic, and educational position in society.

sociogenic hypothesis—An etiological theory that holds that because living in poverty is stressful, one's risk for developing a mental disorder is increased in lower socioeconomic status levels.

spectrum approach—An approach to psychological disorders in which all behavior is viewed on a continuum, rather than in categories.

stereotyped—Repetitive, automatic behaviors.

stereotype—A set of beliefs or associations automatically associated with certain groups of people.

thalidomide—A prescription drug, previously given to pregnant women, which has been linked to severe physical and psychological problems.

theory of mind—A concept in developmental psychology that refers to the ability to understand that someone else may have a different point of view than one's own.

twin studies—Comparisons of heredity rates of certain conditions in monozygotic twins to those of dizygotic twins. Used to determine estimates of genetic contribution of an illness or behavior.

FURTHER RESOURCES

Books and Articles

Grandin, Temple. *Thinking in Pictures: and Other Reports from My Life with Autism.* New York: Vintage, 1996.

Grandin, Temple, and Margaret M. Scariano *Emergence: Labeled Autistic.* New York: Warner Books, 1996.

Haddon, Mark. *The Curious Incident of the Dog in the Night-time.* New York: Doubleday, 2003.

Robison, John Elder. *Look Me in the Eye: My Life with Asperger's.* New York: Three Rivers Press, 2008.

Tammet, Daniel. *Born on a Blue Day: Inside the Extraordinary Mind of an Autistic Savant.* New York: Free Press, 2007.

Web Sites

Autism Research Institute: Autism is Treatable
http://www.autism.com

Autism Speaks
http://www.autismspeaks.org

Defeat Autism Now! (DAN)
http://www.defeatautismnow.com

Generation Rescue
http://www.generationrescue.org

The Judge Rotenberg Center—Residential Treatment Center Treating Behavior Disorders and Developmental Disabilities
http://www.judgerc.org

National Institute of Mental Health
http://www.nimh.nih.gov

milieu therapy, 17
monozygotic twins (MZ), 36–37
Montessori school, 33
Mother Warriors: A Nation of Parents Healing Autism Against All Odds (McCarthy), 67
mutations, 39–40
MZ. *See* monozygotic twins

NAAR. *See* National Alliance for Autism Research
National Alliance for Autism Research (NAAR), 87
National Institute of Mental Health, 2, 61
negative reinforcement, 51
neurons, vi
neuroscientists, vii, ix
neurotransmitter, vi
neurotypical world, 22
New York State Board of Education, 60
NIMH. *See* National Institute of Mental Health
Nobody, Nowhere (Williams), 44–47
Northeastern University, 89

operant conditioning, 51

Peek, Kim, 8–9
peer-reviewed journals, 52
Perner, Josef, 19
perspective taking, 73
pervasive developmental disorders, 6
play therapy, 66
positive reinforcement, 51
pragmatics, 58
prenatal environment, 37
primary genes, 36
prodigious savant, 8
proteins, viii
psychiatric diagnosis, 25–27, 30–31
psychiatrists, vii
psychologists, vii

psychopharmacological treatment, 61–63
punishment, 51

Rain Man, 8
Ramachandran, Vilayanur S., 30
"refrigerator mother," 17, 43
relationships, 2
research, 89–90
Rett's disorder, 7
risperidone, 61
Ritalin, 61
Robison, John, 10, 76–77
Robison Service Company, J.E., 77
rubella. *See* German measles

savant syndrome, 8–9, 56
science-based education, 90
schizophrenia, 15, 40, 50, 61, 85
Schopler, Eric, 55
scientific information, 52–53
Sebat, Jonathan, 39
secondary autism, 38
secondary genes, 36
secretin, 64
seizures, 62
selective serotonin reuptake inhibitors (SSRIs), 61
self-injurious behavior, 61
sensation-seeking behavior, 27
sensory integration disorder, 64
sensory integration therapy, 64–65, 70
shock therapy. *See* electro-convulsive treatment
Skinner, B.F., 51, 53, 59
social interactions, 5
Social Security Disability Insurance (SSDI), 24
social services, 21, 24
social skills
    Asperger syndrome, 71–72
    impaired, 3, 11–12, 48–49, 81
    loss of, 7

social skills, improved, 52
social skills training, 73, 75, 76–78
socioeconomic level, 43
socioeconomic status, 40, 42–43
sociogenic hypothesis, 40
sound-color synesthesia, 28
spectrum approach, 10
spectrum disorder, defined, 72
Splinter skills, 8
spontaneous mutations, 43
"squeeze box." *See* "hug machine"
SSDI. *See* Social Security Disability
    Insurance
SSI. *See* Supplemental Security Income
SSRIs. *See* selective serotonin reuptake
    inhibitors
St. Georges Hospital Medical School
    (London, England), 75
stereotype, 25
stereotyped, 7
stroke, 29
Supplemental Security Income (SSI), 24
supplements, 64
susceptibility genes, 36
synapses, viii
synesthesia, 9, 28–30

talented savant, 8
Tammet, Daniel, 9
TEACCH. *See* Treatment and
    Education of Autistic and Related
    Communication-handicapped
    Children.
temporal lobe epilepsy, 29, 30
thalidomide, 38

theory of mind, 18–19
toxic environmental, 37
toxins, 89
Treatment and Education of Autistic and
    Related Communication-handicapped
    Children (TEACCH), 55–59
treatment of autism. *See* autism,
    treatment
treatment-resistant mood disorder, 50
Treffert, Darold, 8
Trinity College (Dublin, Ireland), 73
Trinity College Cambridge, 30
twin study, 36–37

University of California—San Diego, 30
University of California, Los Angeles, 53
University of Chicago, 17, 25, 37
University of Illinois, 24
University of North Carolina, Chapel Hill,
    55–56
University of Wisconsin—Madison
    Medical School, 8
U.S. Food and Drug Administration
    (FDA), 61

vaccines, 13, 38, 82
vitamin B6, 64

Williams, Donna, 44–47
Wimmer, Heinz, 19
Wright, Bob, 87
Wright, Susan, 87

Yee, Kenny, 39–40

ABOUT THE AUTHOR

Heather Barnett Veague received her B.A. from the University of California, Los Angeles and her Ph.D. from Harvard University. She is the author of several journal articles about mental illness and three other books in this *Psychological Disorders* series. She is currently the Director of Clinical Research in the Laboratory for Adolescent Studies at Vassar College. Dr. Veague lives in Massachusetts with her husband and children.